Who's the Fairest of Them All?

WHO'S THE FAIREST
OF THEM ALL?

The Truth about Opportunity, Taxes,
and Wealth in America

STEPHEN MOORE

ENCOUNTER BOOKS • *New York* • *London*

First American edition published in 2012 by Encounter Books,
an activity of Encounter for Culture and Education, Inc.,
a nonprofit, tax exempt corporation.
Encounter Books website address: www.encounterbooks.com

Manufactured in the United States and printed on
acid-free paper. The paper used in this publication meets
the minimum requirements of ANSI/NISO Z39.48Ð1992
(R 1997) (Permanence of Paper).

FIRST AMERICAN EDITION

LIBRARY OF CONGRESS CATALOGING-IN-PUBLICATION DATA

Moore, Stephen, 1960-
Who's the fairest of them all? : the truth about opportunity, taxes, and
wealth in America / Stephen Moore.
p. cm.
Includes bibliographical references .
ISBN 978-1-59403-684-2 (hardcover : alk. paper) -- ISBN 978-1-59403-685-9
(ebook)
1. United States--Economic policy. 2. Fiscal policy--United States.
3. Equality--United States. 4. Taxation--United States.
5. Rich people--Taxation--United States. 6. Income distribution--United
States. I. Title.
HC106.84.M66 2012
332.600973--dc23
2012024480

Contents

Not since the 1930s has the issue of class warfare been more front and center in the policy debate in Washington. President Obama is seeking higher tax rates on capital gains, dividends, estates, small business owners, and "the rich." He is not promoting these ideas to enhance economic growth—they are anti-growth policies—but to advance the concept of fairness. If economic growth isn't the goal, we shouldn't be surprised if this agenda doesn't generate it. But it is worse than that—unless it is reversed, this agenda will set in motion the largest tax hike in decades beginning on January 1, 2013. I know of no economic theory that would predict this policy will make America more prosperous.

The current fairness rhetoric from the White House is an unfortunate misplacement of attention; the key policy task is to restore robust and resilient economic growth—which will make all Americans better off. While industriousness, hard work, and grit have traditionally been virtues respected by all Americans, too many commentators diminish this virtue by dividing society into the "haves" and the "have-nots," then assigning blame to this outcome on businesspeople. Worse, success, risk-taking, and entrepreneurship—vital for growth and job creation—are vilified.

My own research, and research by many scholars, supports the major findings of this book—that low tax rates, the free enterprise system, and steady economic growth are the best tools to improve Americans' economic condition. High tax rates, especially on investment and saving, reduce growth, which means less economic opportunity for those who start at the lowest rungs of the economic ladder. We can avoid high tax rates with an emphasis on spending restraint and tax reform that would reduce marginal tax rates.

It is important to get the history right, too. Restraints on taxes and spending in the 1980s and 1990s did not shrink the ranks of middle-income Americans, as some argue today. Indeed, they helped to make middle-income individuals as a group better off and helped increase the income and wealth of many. This is called upward economic mobility. And this upward climb is not enhanced by attacking the well-off, but through greater competition and opportunity.

In the past several years, concerns about upward mobility have rightly been raised, in part thanks to a severe recession and the anemic recovery. The combination of failure to confront the nation's long-term fiscal challenges and increased policy uncertainty have retarded private-sector growth. Even in 2011, as the economy was technically growing, median after-tax income fell. No wonder so many Americans believe we are still in recession.

The debate about higher taxes and income inequality and the role of government versus free enterprise in distributing income is likely to dominate the policy debate in the months and years ahead. To prepare voters for the important choices they must make that debate based on facts and evidence, not half-baked truths sprinkled with catchy lingo about "fairness," "equality," "greed," "the 1 percent versus the 99 percent," and "tax cuts for the rich."

Many of the stubborn facts about taxes, income growth, and wealth are contained in this book and many of them may surprise readers. That the rich don't pay their fair share is by now a Washington staple. That the richest 1 percent pays almost 40 percent of income taxes—as reported by the IRS—may to many appear to be a closely guarded secret.

This book, then, and its array of economic statistics is a step toward informing the debate the nation must have. If Americans familiarize themselves with facts, they will be better-informed voters. And in that case, the odds are high that voters will choose policies that create a new rising tide of prosperity in America that lifts our prosperity and our children's prosperity.

Glenn Hubbard, Columbia University

CHAPTER 1

THE POVERTY OF EQUALITY

The year was 2081, and everybody was finally equal. They weren't only equal before God and the law. They were equal every which way. Nobody was smarter than anybody else. Nobody was better looking than anybody else. Nobody was stronger or quicker than anybody else. All this equality was due to the 211th, 212th and 213th Amendments to the Constitution, and to the unceasing vigilance of agents of the United States Handicapper General.

So began Kurt Vonnegut's 1961 short story "Harrison Bergeron." [1] In that brave, new world, the government forced each individual to wear "handicaps" to offset any advantage they had, so that everyone could be truly and fully equal. Beautiful people had to wear ugly masks to hide their good looks. The strong had to wear compensating weights to slow them down. Graceful dancers were burdened with bags of bird shot. Those with above-average intelligence had to wear government transmitters in their ears that would emit sharp noises every twenty seconds shattering their thoughts "to keep them... from taking unfair advantage of their brains." [2]

But Harrison Bergeron was a special problem, because he was so far above average in everything. Vonnegut explained, "Nobody had ever borne heavier handicaps.... Instead of a little ear radio for a mental handicap, he wore a tremendous pair of earphones, and spectacles with thick wavy lenses." [3] Seven feet tall, "Scrap metal was hung all over him" to offset his strength, to the point that "Harrison looked like a walking junkyard." [4]

---

1 Kurt Vonnegut, "Harrison Bergeron," *Welcome to the Monkey House*
  (New York: The Dial Press, 2006).
2 Ibid., p. 7.
3 Ibid., p. 11.
4 Ibid.

The youthful Harrison did not accept these burdens easily, so he had been jailed. But with his myriad advantages and talents, he had broken out. An announcement on TV explained the threat, "He is a genius and an athlete...and should be regarded as extremely dangerous." [5]

Harrison broke into a TV studio, which was broadcasting the performance of a troupe of dancing ballerinas. On national television, he illegally cast off each one of his handicaps. Then he did the same for one of the ballerinas, and then the orchestra, which he commanded to play. To shockingly beautiful chords, Harrison and the ballerina began to dance. Vonnegut explained the beauty of their dance,

> *Not only were the laws of the land abandoned, but the laws of gravity and the laws of motion as well.... The studio ceiling was thirty feet high, but each leap brought the dancers nearer to it. It became their obvious intention to kiss the ceiling. They kissed it. And then, neutralizing gravity with love and pure will, they remained suspended in air inches below the ceiling, and they kissed each other for a long, long time.* [6]

Social safety nets to provide a floor of help for the needy and to alleviate human suffering are easily justifiable on moral grounds. Nearly everyone supports them to prevent severe hardship for those disabled, or widowed, or orphaned, or even just temporarily down on their luck. In modern and wealthy societies like ours, there is broad voter consent to such policies that ensure that people do not suffer from deprivation of the necessities of life: food, shelter, and clothing. This recognizes that we have a moral obligation to help our fellow man. How much of that should be done with private charity and how much should be done with government taxation and distribution is always an open question. And the truth is, such safety nets designed to rely on modern markets and incentives, and focused on the truly needy, would not be costly, in proportion to the immense wealth of our society.

---

5 Ibid., p. 10.
6 Ibid., p. 13.

But once such policies are established, going beyond them to take from some by force of law what they have produced and consequently earned, to give to others merely for the purpose of making incomes and wealth more equal is not justifiable. Vonnegut's story helps to explain.

Why not? First, because achieving true and comprehensive equality would involve violations of personal liberty, as the talented and capable must be prevented from using their abilities and advantages to get ahead of others. Under this philosophy, the more productive must be treated punitively through high tax rates simply because they used their abilities to produce more than others. What we have just described is a progressive tax system. Work and produce a little bit and we take 10 percent. Work and produce more and we take 20 percent, and so on, with some societies taking as much as 90 percent of the output. The United States did so after World War II, with 90 percent marginal tax rates.

In a society where men and women were angels and always put the welfare of others ahead of themselves, this system—from each according to their ability, to each according to their needs—might even work. High tax rates wouldn't have any negative consequences, because everyone would work for everyone else's benefit. Society would be like one large commune with everyone working for the common good. The ambitious, hard worker would get the same as the one who sleeps in and lives a lazy lifestyle. Output would be high and we would have almost complete equality of outcome.

The problem, of course, is that men and women are not angels. We are driven by self-interest. Not entirely, of course, but enough to severely deter work incentives by giving everyone an equal share despite their contribution. This is why in all those places that have tried to enforce the more extreme vision of mandatory equality, totalitarian governments have emerged with very poor citizens. And by the way, in practice these societies are not very equal either. Richer and freer countries tend to have smaller income disparities than poorer and less free nations.

Moreover, as Vonnegut's story illustrates, inequalities of wealth and income are not the only important differences in society. If equality is truly a moral obligation, then inequalities of beauty, intelligence, strength, grace, talent, etc., logically all should be leveled as well. That would require some rather heavy-handed government control and intervention. It is not fair that LeBron James has a 48-inch vertical leap and I have 4-inch vertical leap. It is not fair that some have high IQs and others have below average ones. It is not fair that Christie Brinkley is beautiful, that some people are born with photographic memories, that one person gets cancer and the next one doesn't. We Americans were born in a land of opportunity and wealth, while billions around the world are born into poverty and squalor. We won the ultimate lottery of life being born in this great and rich country. Where is the justice in that?

The goal of a society should not be and cannot be to make people equal in outcomes. It cannot happen given the individual attributes we were each endowed with by our creator. And it is the opposite of justice and fairness to try to equalize outcomes based on those attributes each of us has. It is not fair to the beautiful to force them to wear ugly masks. It is not fair to the strong to punish them by holding them down with excess weights. It is not fair to the graceful and athletic to deprive them of their talents. In the same way, it is not fair to the productive, to the risk takers, to the hard-working, to deprive them of what they have produced, merely to make them equal to others who have worked less, taken less risk, and produced less. As Vonnegut's story shows, putting social limits on the success that people are allowed to achieve with their own talents and abilities makes everyone worse off, because it deprives society of the benefits from their brilliance and beauty and skills and talents. The fact that Bill Gates and Steve Jobs made billions of dollars in income—more than some whole societies make—has on paper made America a more unequal society. But is the middle class better or worse off for Microsoft and Apple products? Should we curse the invention of the personal computer that is now in nearly every home in America simply because it made these men unthinkably wealthy? Since hundreds of millions of people buy their products willingly, it would seem self-evident that Mr. Gates and Mr. Jobs generated a better world for everyone, not just themselves.

Finally, this vision of equality as a social goal, with equal incomes and wealth for all, is severely counterproductive economically, and so makes for a poor society as well. Pursuing such a vision would require very high marginal tax rates on anyone with above average production, income, and wealth, which experience as well as theory shows leads to less production. As we saw in our discussion of tax policy above, the less the productive are allowed to keep of what they produce, the less they will produce.

A good and just tax system should be designed to make the poor rich, not the rich poor. The preoccupation with equality sometimes leads to policies that get that objective reversed, as when Barack Obama says we should raise the capital gains rate even if it doesn't raise revenues for the government, for "the purpose of fairness." How is an outcome that hurts everyone fair?

And it's easy to think of other unfavorable outcomes from this fairness fetish. Under the social justice of equal income and wealth for all, investment would make no sense at all. Investment is made only to earn returns, which means more income. Anyone who invests more than others would have an above average income, which would be expropriated to the extent it was above the same average income as anyone else receives. But if you invest less than others on average, and suffer a below average income, you would be rewarded with a grant from the government to ensure you enjoyed the same average income as everyone else. So, again, the only rational strategy for everyone would be to avoid all investment.

China is one good recent example. During the era of communism in the 1940s, '50s, and '60s, when all land was cultivated for the "common good," and the food was evenly distributed to all, regardless of how much one worked, the Chinese society produced way too little food and many millions of Chinese people, including children, starved to death. But starting in the 1980s, agriculture reforms began to emerge, allowing farmers to take a small plot of land and keep the food that was grown on those properties. An amazing thing happened. Production of food, even on these very small tracts of land, surged—multiples higher than the output on the communal lands. Chinese farmers who owned the land themselves and owned the crops that were grown on that land, saw output levels double and even triple from the previous arrangement where all food was put in a communal pot. Private ownership of the farms led to a green revolution in China, with this nation quickly becoming a food exporter.

Was this because the Chinese people are selfish and don't care about their fellow man? No, the Chinese are no more selfish than other cultures. It's just that human beings are hardwired to first put our own well-being and that of our kids above that of the fellow we don't even know. The human pursuit of happiness begins for most by taking care of ourselves and our families first and that is deeply ingrained into our core.

I would add that the alternative course of demanding equality of opportunity can (and almost always does in practice) lead to the subordination of other values, such as personal liberty. As one example, the talented almost always want to leave a society where their talents are suppressed. Think of North Korea or Cuba or East Germany after World War II. So these regimes quickly discovered that to keep their nations from economic collapse, they had to enforce tight restrictions on emigration and international travel to avoid losing their most productive citizens. And it wasn't just the best and brightest who wanted to leave. Many average citizens wanted to flee from an economically stagnant, poor society. So the governments had to restrict everyone from leaving, imposing on the liberty of all. This is where the Berlin Wall came from. It was not a wall to keep invaders out. It was to keep the citizens captive.

But doesn't the Declaration of Independence itself say that "All men are created equal"? And isn't equal justice and liberty for all, indeed, a fundamental American ideal? What is involved in these expressions, however, is a different concept of equality than the social justice concept of equal incomes and wealth for all.

The original and traditionally American concept of equality is "equality under the law." That means the same rules apply to all, not the same results. Baseball is a fair game because the same rules apply to all players.

Equality of rules equally protects the property of all, which encourages savings, investment, and work, because all are assured of the same protection for the fruits of their work and productive activities. Equality of rules ensures that all enjoy the same freedom of contract, empowering them to maximize value and production, and plan investment knowing they can rely on their agreed contractual rights. Equality of rules provides a framework in which all are equally free to pursue their individual vision of happiness to the maximum.

Within this framework of equal rules for all, the outcome of the market in terms of income and wealth is fair, for two fundamental reasons. The first is that people basically earn in the market the value of what they produce. Economists say more formally that wages equal the marginal productivity of labor. That encompasses both the concept of the market value of the output of each worker, and the number of workers that can do the same thing. If the worker's output is unique, that output will be worth more, to the extent that people value it, because only he can produce it. James Patterson has gotten rich writing mystery/thriller books that the public buys over and over because they derive happiness from reading his writing and are captivated by his plots. Every one of us can sing, but only Katy Perry has a string of number one hits that young people all over the world want to listen to over and over.

Alex Rodriguez and LeBron James each make a lot more money than any teacher, or any doctor. In a broad social sense, what teachers do and what doctors do is worth a lot more than what Alex Rodriguez and LeBron James do. Not everyone can do what teachers do, and fewer still can do what doctors do. But only Alex Rodriguez and LeBron James can do what they do. What they do pleases millions every night of the long season that each plays, in person at the stadium, on the radio, on television, in the paper in the morning. Each fan is willing to pay a little in return for their unique performance. Since they are each the only ones who can provide that performance, what they get adds up to a large amount for each. What they get is not unfair. They earn it, through talent, hard work, and performance.

This is why it is even wrong to speak of the "distribution" of income and wealth. Income and wealth are not distributed. Income and wealth are produced, and in a fair society they come into the world attached to the rightful owner that produced them. As the late Harvard philosophy professor Robert Nozick wrote, "Whoever makes something, having bought or contracted for all other held resources used in the process…is entitled to it. The situation is *not* one of something's getting made, and there being an open question of who is to get it." If income and wealth are not attached to the owner that produced them, they tend not to be created at all.

Second, what is produced is not taken from anyone else. It is created by the worker. So the income and wealth that such production earns does not come at the expense of anyone else. It is created by the earner. The economy is not a fixed pie with slices being handed out by Barack Obama. Each worker expands the pie, creating his own slices.

The end result of a society that puts equality ahead of freedom and prosperity is an unhappy one. As we have seen throughout history, high tax rates, high welfare benefits, and collectivist outcomes lead to deprivation and poverty. We want a fair society where everyone can realize their fullest human potential. And yes that means that some—Bill Gates, Michael Jordan, Tom Cruise, Albert Pujols, Lady Gaga, and Sergey Brin—will get a lot richer than others. There is no injustice in that.

We left until now the thrilling ending of Mr. Vonnegut's story. At the very moment when Harrison Bergeron and the ballet dancer were thrilling the crowds with their expertise and their breathtaking talents, as the orchestra was breaking into shockingly beautiful chords, and the crowd's cheers reached a crescendo of joy and admiration, in barged the Handicapper General, Diana Moon Glampers. With a double-barreled shotgun she shot the two lawbreakers dead, and equality was restored.

CHAPTER 2

HOW DO WE CREATE
A FAIR SOCIETY?

President Obama has declared that the standard by which all policies and policy outcomes are judged is fairness. He declared in 2012, "We've sought to ensure that every citizen can count on some basic measure of security. We do this because we recognize that no matter how responsibly we live our lives, any one of us, at any moment, might face hard times, might face bad luck, might face a crippling illness or a layoff." [1] And that, he says, is why we have a social safety net. He says that returning to a standard of fairness where anyone can get ahead through hard work is the "issue of our time." And perhaps it is.

This book explores what it means for our economic system and our economic results to be "fair." Does it mean that everyone has a fair shot? Does it mean that everyone gets the same amount of everything? Does it mean the government can assert the authority to forcibly take from the successful and give to the poor? Is government supposed to be like Robin Hood determining who gets what? Or should the market decide that?

Before we answer those questions, we first should recognize that just about everyone wants to raise the incomes and living standards of the poor (I sure do). Inarguably, a top priority of U.S. economic policy should be to help expand opportunities and raise the earnings of those stuck at the bottom. It's been said that the measure of a society's compassion and the effectiveness of its economic policies is how well the poor fare in society. That in a nation of such affluence, there are still some forty million Americans living in poverty today

---

1 "Remarks by the President at the Associated Press Luncheon," April 3, 2012, http://www.whitehouse.gov/the-press-office/2012/04/03/remarks-president-associated-press-luncheon.

is a travesty and a failure of our economic and civic institutions
And what would be even worse is if children who are born into
poverty cannot escape it as an adult. We all still want to believe in the
quintessential American Horatio Alger story, of the poor man who
pulls himself up with hard work and becomes rich. And fortunately,
we see in immigrants who come with nothing and rise up that the
economic ladder is still there, though maybe it doesn't rise high
enough for enough of our citizens.

The issue is: How do we make sure that the middle class and the
poor can get ahead and address this societal shortcoming? The left
argues that conservatives don't care about poor people, and this is why
they oppose income redistribution in tax policy, welfare payments to
the poor, higher budgets for social programs, regulations like higher
minimum wages, and so on.

But one of premises of this book is that it is equally (maybe even
more) plausible to say that liberals don't care about poor people. The
welfare state has trapped generations in poverty. Liberals opposed
welfare reform when it was a great success in lifting the incomes of the
poor. High tax rates are not an effective way to redistribute income. The
minimum wage eliminates jobs for those at the bottom. The left defends
inner city schools, but those dismally performing schools have done as
much as anything to hold back the economic progress of the poor. The
dissolution of the black family, in part, because of welfare, has forced
several generations of black children to be reared in fatherless homes,
which is a prescription for trouble later in life. Solve these thorny
problems and you go a long way toward solving the inequality.

It is a myth that the left is more "compassionate" than the right
and it is wrong for those who believe in the free enterprise system
and who oppose more government spending on income transfer
programs to surrender the moral high ground. Liberal solutions
all too often disserve the people they are allegedly designed to help.
Even if the liberals who set up these programs had their hearts in the
right place, it doesn't make up for the harm they have done to the goal
of achieving financial independence for the poor. Good intentions
are not enough. We need positive results. And throwing money at a
problem is not sufficient and in many cases it is counterproductive.

In America today we have forty-five million Americans on
food stamps at a cost of $75 billion. That is about one-in-seven
Americans. It is nearly three times as many on the food dole as in
2000. But is the program lifting Americans out of poverty or keeping
them there? As Charles Murray once put it, the tragedy of the $10
trillion welfare state is not how much it cost, but how little it bought.

There is an old saying: Give a man a fish and he eats for a day.
Teach a man to fish and he eats for a lifetime. We are exercising false
compassion when we give handouts without a hand up to get people
out of their state of dependency. And yet in 2012, Barack Obama was
trying to eviscerate work-for-welfare programs.

For years the left has argued, "But why can't we be more like
progressive Europe, which has a super-generous welfare state? The
safety net covers people from cradle to grave. It gives five weeks of
vacation, free health care, early retirement, free day care, no-layoff
rules to protect workers, and on and on. Workers in France now
get additional paid vacation if they get sick on their vacation. The
workers support the nonworkers." But that model has imploded
right before our very eyes. Greece, Italy, Spain, Portugal, and France
are melting down. Sweden has always been held up as the socialist
welfare state paradigm. And Sweden is doing relatively well today.
But they are dismantling, not building up, their welfare state
policies. As they move toward markets, the citizenry has seen their
economic circumstances improve. This was an act of compassion,
not an act of greed or selfishness.

Even here in America, we have had plenty of experience with
giving people an equal amount. The ramifications of such policies
have not been pretty. The original experiment of evenly distributing
the gains and production from the economy came during the earliest
days of the colonists from Europe who tried to settle here in a new
world. The story is retold by the folks at the Ludwig Von Mises
Institute who chronicled this important history lesson.[2]

"In his *History of Plymouth Plantation*, the governor of the colony,
William Bradford, reported that the colonists went hungry for years,

---

2 Richard J. Maybury, "The Great Thanksgiving Hoax," November 20, 1999,
   http://mises.org/daily/336/.

because they refused to work in the fields. They preferred instead to steal food. He says the colony was riddled with 'corruption,' and with 'confusion and discontent.' The crops were small because 'much was stolen both by night and day, before it became scarce eatable.'"

Because of the sharing of output and the incentive of idleness of workers, the first "Thanksgiving," did not deliver the feast of modern mythology. Rather, that period was marked by hunger, and sometimes death from starvation.

It was this era of scarcity and depravity that led to a new economic model to encourage labor and individual initiative. Within a few years, food output grew in abundance. According to the Von Mises Institute's analysis, "in 1624 so much food was produced that the colonists were able to begin exporting corn." The authors describe the joyous turnaround this way: "After the poor harvest of 1622, writes Bradford, 'they began to think how they might raise as much corn as they could, and obtain a better crop.' They began to question their form of economic organization. This had required that 'all profits & benefits that are got by trade, working, fishing, or any other means' were to be placed in the common stock of the colony, and that, 'all such persons as are of this colony, are to have their meat, drink, apparel, and all provisions out of the common stock.' A person was to put into the common stock all he could, and take out only what he needed."

This was the first repudiation of socialism and collectivism in the new land. Bradford wrote "that 'young men that are most able and fit for labor and service' complained about being forced to 'spend their time and strength to work for other men's wives and children.'" It was not just a shortage of food that resulted from the sharing of output. Clothing and other supplies were not to be had because of inadequate incentives to produce them.

Again, according to the Von Mises Institute's telling of the tale: "To rectify this situation, in 1623 Bradford abolished socialism. He gave each household a parcel of land and told them they could keep what they produced, or trade it away as they saw fit. In other words, he replaced socialism with a free market, and that was the end of famines. Many early groups of colonists set up socialist states, all with the same terrible results. At Jamestown, established in 1607, out of every shipload of settlers that arrived, less than half would survive their first twelve months in America. Most of the work was being done by only one-fifth of the men, the other four-fifths choosing to be parasites. In the winter of 1609-10, called 'The Starving Time,' the population fell from five-hundred to sixty."

What saved the day was free market capitalism. Food was plentiful and industry flourished. The settlers had learned a valuable lesson about how to make everyone in the community better off with more of everything. And it wasn't by taking from productive Peter to give to unproductive Paul. It was by allowing Peter to keep most if not all of the fruits of his labor. That is the real Thanksgiving story. It is a celebration of the horns of plenty from capitalism and a rejection of the poverty of collectivism. The nation's economy tends to falter—as it is faltering now—when that lesson is from time to time, ignored.

In reciting this history, one has to wonder what today's liberal progressives would have thought about all this. Would economists from the University of California at Berkeley decry the riches of the biggest producers? Would Barack Obama have complained that the income divide grew wider because of the increase in output? Everyone may have been made better off by moving toward capitalism, but not at equal and maybe not even at a "fair" pace.

By the way, history is full of such examples. But here we are in 2012, and not only is public welfare viewed as necessary, but also as a stimulant to the economy. Rep. Steny Hoyer recently asserted that the economists he listens to say that the two best ways to stimulate the economy are to expand unemployment insurance and food stamps. Sounds like Mr. Hoyer needs a new group of economists.

GROWTH AND FAIRNESS

To be against income redistribution or socialist policies that don't work in practice is not to be hard-hearted but to be sensible and wise. It is not to say that we must live in a dog-eat-dog society where everyone looks out for number one. Americans are the most charitable and benevolent people on earth and we give sometimes even when it hurts. But giving voluntarily and having your output taken from you are entirely different things. A study by Arthur Brooks of the American Enterprise Institute finds that private charitable dollars are multiple times more effective in helping the poor than public programs. That is in part because private charity often requires some change in the behavior of the person receiving the aid, such as getting off drugs, working for the aid, or helping others. Public charity almost never attaches these conditions.

One practical argument against redistribution is that forced sharing inevitably leads to special benefits to a few insiders. Those in power soon believe that they are more deserving than the governed. This leads to the opposite of fairness: special and unearned benefits to the ruling class, not based on what they contribute, but based on their political power.

The argument we hear today over and over is that if we take from the rich who have so much, and do so through high tax rates, we can help the poor. President Obama says these rich people—the millionaires and billionaires—"don't need the money." So this evidently gives license to the government to take it. In reality, a lesson that permeates this book is that high tax rates stifle individual initiative, chase capital and businesses away, and often hurt the poor the most. The rich in America are generally business owners and investors. I show later in this book that output is usually higher when tax rates are lower. So high tax rates may lead to more equality, but at the price of less growth and less to divide.

By giving to the poor unconditionally, we also erect a roadblock— spiritually and economically—to more productive activities. Self- respect, dignity, and fulfillment in work aren't achieved by receiving a handout. More important, government handouts can often impede the work process. Harvard economist Robert Barro reviewed why the economic recovery under President Obama was so slow from 2009– 2012. He found that one impediment to growth was "the expansion of the social safety net programs, including food stamps, unemployment insurance, Medicaid and housing assistance programs." In a study published by the National Bureau of Economic Research, University of Chicago economist Casey Mulligan observed that because these programs were means tested (falling or ending as income rises), expanding them raises the effective tax rate on labor income. Mr. Mulligan estimated that "the marginal tax rate for low income households went from around 40 percent in 2007 to about 48 percent in 2009 when the recovery began." These programs diluted the incentive to work and in economics, incentives are what matter most.

The same effect was observed in a study by Michael Tanner and me in 1995. [3] Welfare benefits in many states were the equivalent of an $8, $10, or in places like Hawaii, up to $12 an hour salary. Why work? And welfare recipients didn't. Welfare caseloads were generally higher where benefit amounts were the highest. Go figure. A lot of that was fixed with work-for-welfare requirements in the 1996 welfare reform bill. That law helped move more than half of all welfare recipients into productive jobs. What a success and a stroke for fairness as many former welfare mothers became productive and moved up the income ladder over time. Ron Haskins of the Brookings Institution found that when work requirements were put in place for welfare, the child poverty rate fell faster than at any time in thirty years. Welfare reform was the most compassionate policy in half a century. Call it tough love, but it worked.

What this book tries to demonstrate with facts and evidence is that the free enterprise system is the on-ramp to economic progress and rising incomes. A Heritage Foundation study on economic progress across the globe finds clear and compelling evidence that the poor are always and everywhere better off in economically free countries than in nations that are not free. So in other words, if we judge society by how well it serves the poor, then free enterprise is far and away the greatest anti-poverty program known to man. The ranks of the poor have risen and the progress of the middle class has stalled in the United States in recent years because we have moved so aggressively away from free markets and toward ham-handed government solutions.

---

3 Michael Tanner, Stephen Moore, and David Hartman, "The Work Versus Welfare Trade-Off: An Analysis of the Total Level of Welfare Benefits by State," Cato Institute, September 1995

Real Fairness

One more point before we move on and examine the evidence and trends in America on taxes, incomes, and wealth.

In an economic speech before the National Press Club in April of 2012,[4] President Obama explained what has gone wrong with the American Dream. He said:

> *What if anything can we do to restore a sense of security for people who are willing to work hard and act responsibly in this country?*
>
> *Can we succeed in a nation where a shrinking number of people do exceedingly well, while a growing number struggle to get by? Or are we better off when everyone gets a fair shot, and everyone does their fair share, and everyone plays by the same rules?*

These are exactly the right questions, though everyone who believes in the free market believes that there should be one set of rules that everyone plays by. Actually, it is government that sets up separate rules for favored players. Many inequities and much of what is unfair in society are a result of government policies that are designed to promote fairness. The remedies are often worse and more corrosive than the disease. This is what Milton Friedman called the law of unintended consequences of governmental policy.

So let's try to gauge the fairness of this president's own policies. To wit:

Is it fair that some companies that produce electricity from wind and solar power and ethanol get hundreds of millions of dollars of subsidies and pay virtually no taxes, while the oil and gas industries that provide twenty times as much energy pay tens of billions of dollars of taxes?

Is it fair that those who work forty, fifty, and in some cases sixty hours a week to make ends meet, have to pay taxes to support an unemployment insurance system that pays those who haven't worked for nearly two years?

---

4 "Remarks by the President at the Associated Press Luncheon," April 3, 2012, http://www.whitehouse.gov/the-press-office/2012/04/03/remarks-president-associated-press-luncheon.

Is it fair that those who took out responsible mortgages and pay them each month on time have to now see their taxes used to subsidize those who acted recklessly, greedily, and in some cases deceitfully, in taking out mortgages they can't afford to repay?

Is it fair that my kids and grandkids and grandkids' kids—who never voted for Obama—will have to pay off the $830 billion stimulus bill and the rest of the $5 trillion of debt accumulated over the past four years?

Is it fair that some twenty thousand workers won't have jobs next year, because the President sided with radical environmentalists and killed the shovel-ready project called the Keystone Pipeline? [5]

Is it fair that big banks got huge government subsidies because they bought trillions of mortgage-backed securities, but the smaller community banks they compete against got nothing?

Is it fair that many of Mr. Obama's largest contributors received federal loan guarantees on their investments in renewable energy projects that went bust?

Is it fair that federal employees receive pay and benefits that are nearly double the pay and benefits of the private sector workers who pay their salaries? [6]

Is it fair that the richest 3 percent of taxpayers now must pay more in federal taxes than the bottom 97 percent—and yet they are disparaged for not paying enough taxes? [7]

Is it fair that we compel tens of millions of young people in America to pay 12 percent of every paycheck into a Social Security system that is running out of money and is likely to offer these workers a negative rate of return on their investment?

Is it fair that American corporations have to pay the highest statutory corporate tax rate of all but one other industrialized nation? [8]

---

5 Alain Sherter, "Keystone pipeline: How many jobs really at stake," CBS News, January 19, 2012, http://www.cbsnews.com/8301-505123_162-57361212/keystone-pipeline-how-many-jobs-really-at-stake/.

6 Chris Edwards, "Overpaid Federal Workers," Cato Institute, August 2012.

7 Peter Ferrara, "Obama's Budget: The Decline and Fall of the American Economy," *Forbes*, February 16, 2012.

8 Chris Isidore, "U.S. corporate tax: No. 1 in the world," *CNN Money*, March 27, 2012.

Is it fair that President Obama is able to send his two daughters to elite private schools that are safer, better run, and produce higher test scores than the Washington DC area's public schools, when millions of other inner city families across America are denied that basic right to choose and must send their kids to rotten schools?

Is it fair that Americans who build a family business, hire workers, reinvest and save their money, and pay a lifetime of often millions of dollars in federal, state, and local taxes, must then pay at the time of their deaths an additional estate tax of 35 percent on what they had hoped to pass on to their children?

Is it fair that the U.S. Treasury Secretary, the former Democratic Senate Majority Leader, and the U.S. Congressional Representative for New York didn't pay all their taxes? [9]

Is it fair that the richest 10 percent of Americans pay a higher share of federal income taxes than do the richest 10 percent in every other industrialized nation? [10]

Is it fair that after the first two years of Obamanomics, the poor are poorer, the middle class has shrunk, and median incomes have fallen?[11]

Is it fair that roughly 90 percent of the reporters who are covering the presidential election are Democrats? [12]

Is it fair that the three counties that have the highest per capita income in America today are all inside the Washington, DC metropolitan area? [13]

---

9 Barry Talei "Reid'em and weep: A leader's shameless slur," *New York Post*, August 8, 2012.
10 Scott A. Hodge "No Country Leans on Upper-Income Households as Much as U.S.," *Tax Foundation*, March 21, 2011 http://taxfoundation.org/blog/no-country-leans-upper-income-households-much-us.
11 James Pethokoukis, "Obama's inequality argument just utterly collapsed," *American Enterprise Institute*, Ausust 13, 2012, http://www.aei-ideas.org/2012/04/obamas-inequality-argument-just-utterly-collapsed/.
12 John Perazzo, "In the Tank: A Statistical Analysis of Media Bias," *Front Page Magazine*, October 31, 2008, http://archive.frontpagemag.com/readArticle. aspx?ARTID=32928.
13 Conor Dougherty, "Incomes Fall in Most Metro Areas," *The Wall Street Journal*, August 10 2010, http://online.wsj.com/article/SB10001424052748703428604575419683851811758.html

Is it fair that soon almost half of the federal budget will take income from young, working people and redistribute it to old, nonworking people that as a group have higher incomes? [14]

Is it fair that in twenty-seven states workers can be compelled to join a union if they want to keep their job? [15]

Is it fair that nearly four out of ten American households now pay *no* federal income tax at all? [16]

There are many more such injustices created by government. Perhaps what is most unfair about our current society is not the inequities created by the marketplace, but the inequities created by the policies of politicians who acted in the name of fairness.

14 Arloc Sherman, Robert Greenstein, and Kathy Ruffing, "Contrary to 'Entitlement Society' Rhetoric, Over Nine-Tenths of Entitlement Benefits Go to Elderly, Disabled, or Working Households," *Center on Budget Policy Priorities*, February 10, 2012, http://www.cbpp.org/cms/?fa=view&id=3677.

15 "Right to Work States Enjoy 'Growth Advantage'," *National Right to Work Newsletter*, April 2012, Volume 58, Number 4.

16 Jeanne Sahadi, "Why half of us don't pay income tax," *CNN Money*, April 26, 2012, http://money.cnn.com/2012/04/26/pf/taxes/income-tax/index.htm.

CHAPTER 3

WHAT HAPPENED TO
THE AMERICAN DREAM?

*We tell people—we tell our kids—that in this country, even if you're born
with nothing, work hard and you can get into the middle class.... And yet,
over the last few decades, the rungs on the ladder of opportunity have
grown farther and farther apart, and the middle class has shrunk.*
—Barack Obama, December 2011, Osawatomie, Kansas

The overarching issue in the 2012 presidential campaign
will be the economic condition of the middle class. Is the
middle class stagnant and held back by the enormous
wealth of the millionaires and billionaires in the top 1
percent? Was the villain Bane, in the latest Batman movie, right,
when he told the residents of Gotham City, "The rich are your
oppressors," as he exhorted the mob to take what the wealthy have,
and as he held kangaroo courts to convict the rich of their alleged
crimes? This has a lot to do with defining what kind of country
America will be in the years and even decades ahead. Will America
be a society driven by opportunity or envy?

Will we put the pursuit of equality ahead of the pursuit of growth?

President Obama has made it clear where he stands. He hopes
to reframe the economic debate, changing it from a story of the
economic meltdown over the past several years and the paltry
recovery, to a story about "fairness" and class division. The Obama
"hope and change" message of 2008 has become a message of "us
versus them"—and by "them," he means the rich and successful.
Mr. Obama drew the class warfare battle lines during a speech in
December 2011 in Osawatomie, Kansas, when he declared that the
middle class pathway to the American dream has been blockaded by
"the breathtaking greed of the few."

The rich got richer, according to Mr. Obama's narrative, by making "huge bets and huge bonuses with other people's money." (He wasn't talking about the folks at Fannie Mae.) Balancing the budget has become nearly impossible, according to Mr. Obama; not because government spending has spiraled out of control—which it quite obviously has under this President's watch—but rather because Republicans won't raise taxes on the much-maligned and supposedly under-taxed, top 1 percent.

The unifier has become the divider. In keeping with this theme of leveling incomes and reducing income gaps, Mr. Obama has embraced even more expensive and expansive government welfare programs, higher taxes on the rich, and more regulation, not less. There are now forty-five million Americans on food stamps, (which is about one in every seven families). That policy agenda is a direct challenge to the free market, low tax ideas that are generally—but not always—espoused by Republicans.

Mr. Obama depicts the political fight as "the defining issue of our time."

Mr. Obama and his left-leaning advisors are telling the electorate that the best way for the middle class and the poor to improve their economic condition is not through hard work, saving, risk-taking, and other economic virtues, but by taking—or stealing—from the gains that the rich have made at everyone else's expense.

It's a radical "Robin Hood" philosophy, but is it based on any real facts about the state of the U.S. economy?

And can an economic strategy of redistributing wealth, rather than one focusing on creating it in the first place, make America a fairer and more prosperous society? This chapter provides answers to these questions. This is a tutorial on trends in taxes, wealth and incomes in America, to help readers decide for themselves what is economically fair and what is economically wise.

But before we dive into the data, let me share with you a recent poll, which I find to be hopeful about what most Americans believe about economic opportunity in America today. Here are the results from a Gallup Poll in December of 2011: "How important is it that the federal government in Washington enacts policies that attempt to do the following?"

This result suggests that growth and equality of opportunity are a much higher priority to American voters than equality of outcomes and leveling incomes. That is reassuring and the evidence on the pages that follow indicates that these instincts are correct.

TRENDS IN INCOME AND WEALTH

Let's start with the big picture of what has happened with the U.S. economy over the last thirty years or so. The premise of the income redistributionists is that this was an era when the fruits of prosperity wentwent almost entirely to the rich, while the poor and middle class hardly made any gains in living standards at all. Is that true?

Table 3.1: December 2011 Gallup Poll Results		
	Very to Extremely Important	**Somewhat to Not Important**
	%	%
Grow and expand the economy	82	18
Increase the equality of opportunity for people to get ahead if they want	70	30
Reduce the income and wealth gap between the rich and the poor	46	54
Gallup: Nov. 28—Dec. 1, 2011		

To answer that, we have to retrace the steps of the economy from the Reagan era through the Obama presidency.

Mr. Obama says that in recent decades the middle class has suffered and shrunk. He is dead wrong on this count. In fact, the last thirty years (up until this recession) have been a boom period for the middle class.

One of the most important lessons of this book is that economic growth is good for all income groups, and stagnation and decline hurt everyone. When the economy declines, the poor get hurt the most. If you're rich and you lose 20 percent of your income, you may have to buy a cheaper car, go out for dinner less often, or cut back on vacation expenses. But if you're poor, even small declines in income may trigger real financial hardship, with less money for the necessities like food, shelter, and healthcare.

Consider what happened in this country in the recessionary 1970s and the go-go 1980s. During the seven-year expansion that lasted from 1982–1989, the economy grew by almost one-third. [1] That is the equivalent of adding the entire economy of West Germany, the third largest in the world at the time, to the U.S. economy. [2] In 1984 alone, real economic growth accelerated by 6.8 percent, the highest in fifty years. [3] Nearly twenty million new jobs were created during this expansion, increasing U.S. civilian employment by almost 20 percent.[4] Unemployment fell to 5.3 percent by 1989, about half of where it stood when the boom began.[5]

Real per capita disposable income increased by 18 percent from 1982–1989, meaning the American standard of living increased by almost 20 percent. [6] Real median family income had fallen during the Carter years, but rebounded in the 1980s. See Figure 3.1. The Carter era decline in income for the bottom 20 percent of income earners was reversed, with average real household income for this group rising by 12.2 percent from 1983–1989.[7] The poverty rate, which had started increasing during the Carter years, declined every year from 1984–1989, dropping by one-sixth from its peak. [8]

The shocking rise in inflation during the Carter years was also reversed. Astoundingly, inflation was reduced by more than half

---

1 Peter Ferrara, "Reaganomics Vs. Obamanomics: Facts and Figures," *Forbes*, June 5, 2011, http://www.forbes.com/sites/peterferrara/2011/05/05/reaganomics-vs-obamanomics-facts-and-figures/.

2 Ibid., p. 4; McKenzie, Richard B. *What Went Right in the 1980s*, (San Francisco: Pacific Research Institute, 1994), p. 8.

3 Arthur B. Laffer, Stephen Moore, and Peter J. Tanous, *The End of Prosperity* (New York: Simon & Schuster, 2008), p. 88.

4 *Economic Report of the President*, January, 1993, Table B-32, p. 385.

5 *Economic Report of the President*, January, 1993, Table 13-69, p. 428.

6 Bartley, *The Seven Fat Years*, p. 4.

7 Ibid., p. 4; McKenzie, Richard B. *What Went Right in the 1980s*, (San Francisco: Pacific Research Institute, 1994), p. 102.

8 *Economic Report of the President*, Table B-28, p. 380.

Figure 3.1: Real Median Family Income, 1970–2010

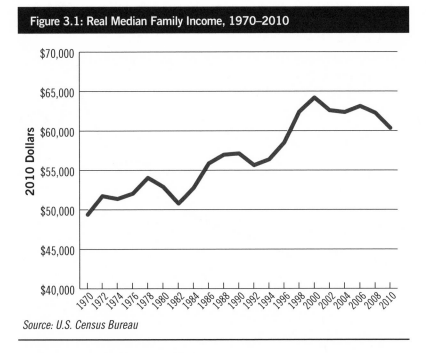

Source: U.S. Census Bureau

from 1980–1982, down to 6.2 percent.[9] It was cut in half again for 1983, to 3.2 percent.[10] The prime rate was cut two-thirds by 1987 to 8.2 percent, on its way down to 6.25 percent by 1992.[11] New home mortgage rates also declined steadily, reaching 9.2 percent by 1988, on their way down to 8 percent by 1992.[12] Note that opponents of the Reagan tax cuts had argued that the cuts would increase interest rates.

Real personal assets rose by nearly $6 trillion, from $15.5 trillion in 1980, to $21.1 trillion in 1990 (an increase of 36 percent).[13] Total real private net worth rose by $4.3 trillion from 1980–1989, totaling $17.1 trillion inconstant dollars (an increase of one-third.[14])

9 *Economic Report of the President*, January, 1993, Table 13-59, p. 462.
10 Ibid.
11 *Economic Report of the President*, January, 1993, Table 13-69, p. 428.
12 Ibid.
13 *Economic Report of the President*, January, 1993, Table 13-69, p. 183.
14 *Economic Report of the President*, Table B-110, p. 473.

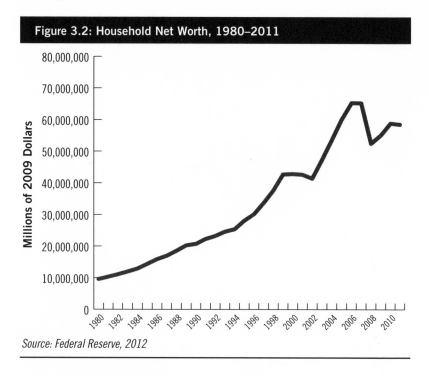

Figure 3.2: Household Net Worth, 1980–2011

Source: Federal Reserve, 2012

The growth spurt that began under Reagan accelerated in the 1990s under Bill Clinton. Another twenty million new jobs were created and incomes grew at an even faster pace in the 1992–1999 expansion. These two decades in particular became an era of almost uninterrupted prosperity. Incomes rose for rich and poor. This was a genuine rising tide that lifted nearly all boats. Over the period 1982–2007, an era I call "the twenty-five year boom," the net worth of Americans rose from roughly $18 trillion to $58 trillion, according to data from the U.S. Federal Reserve Bank. Never before has the nation seen so much wealth creation in such a brief span of history. More financial wealth was created in this twenty-five-year boom than in the previous two hundred years. See Figure 3.2.

Clearly the trend in the 1980s and 1990s was one of rapid growth in output, incomes, and wealth. The country got a lot richer at an unprecedented pace. This is clearly inconsistent with the Obama theme of decline and lost ground.

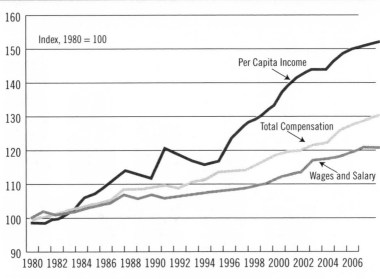

Figure 3.3: Worker Well-Being, 1982–2007

Index, 1980 = 100

Per Capita Income

Total Compensation

Wages and Salary

Source: Based on data from the Census Bureau and the Department of Labor.

ASSESSING THE WINNERS AND LOSERS

The key question is: Who benefited the most and the least from all this growth? The critics argue that the lion's share of the gains went to those people with yachts, Rolls Royces, diamond chandeliers, and Lear jets. But the evidence suggests a broader prosperity that benefited most Americans.

Figure 3.3 shows what happened with three measures of middle class well-being from 1982–2007. The first measure is reported income, mostly wages and salaries. We see here that the median family had a real income gain of about 22 percent based on Census Bureau data. This isn't spectacular, but it is a positive improvement, and it is certainly not "wage stagnation."

This wage and salary data fails to measure other forms of compensation of value to workers that they received from their employers and from their work effort. One of the major trends of the last several decades is that more workers get a larger share of their "pay" in the form of non-wage and salary benefits. These include

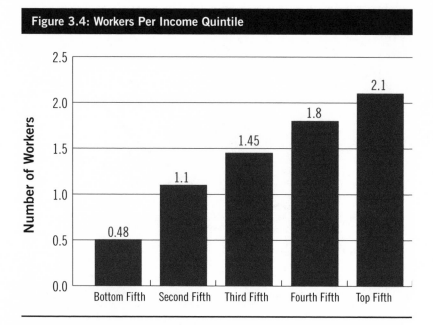

Figure 3.4: Workers Per Income Quintile

everything from health insurance, to pension benefits, tuition assistance, day care, more paid holidays and vacation days, and other benefits that employers provide their workforce.

When we take those benefits into account, we see in Figure 3.3 that total worker compensation is up 33 percent after inflation. (All figures in this chapter are adjusted for inflation. That is, they take account of inflation, unless otherwise indicated.) That one-third increase in total worker compensation in just twenty-five years is a big gain. Throughout most of human history it took a century or more to see gains this large. We can argue about whether these gains were fast enough, but it is false to say families have not made real economic progress over the past three decades.

But we're not done yet. Next we measure per capita income in America. That surged by 51 percent in twenty-five years. That is an almost miraculous rise in the standard of living for American families. Admittedly, this is an average income of *all* families, not a *median* income measure. Since the gains to the rich were larger than the gains by those beneath them on the income scale, this doesn't give us a complete picture of how the middle class fared. If a hundred families saw no income gain at all, but one family saw its income doubled from $5 million to $10 million, the average income gain for that community would be very high, even though all the gains went to one family. But at least this gives us a sense of how much the total income of the U.S. economy expanded during these years.

THE MIDDLE CLASS BOOM

Now we have to probe more deeply into the tricky question of whether the gains over this period were widely shared or just "trickled down" from the ice caps of wealth at the top of the income pyramid.

Democrats, the *New York Times*, and much of the rest of the media say that the gains were not evenly distributed and that this was a gilded age for the super wealthy with few advances for everyone else. Barbara Ehrenreich wrote a book alleging that this was a period when the middle class and poor got "nickle and dimed" while the wealthy amassed fortunes. We hear in the press popular statistics such as "60 percent of the gains went to 1 percent of the families."

This is a distortion of what really happened with family incomes for the bulk of Americans over the past three decades. One of the top scholars on income growth and the well-being of the middle class in America is Richard Burkhauser, an economist at Cornell University and a senior fellow at the well-respected American Enterprise Institute. Mr. Burkhauser examined the data that some scholars use to suggest flat incomes for the middle class since the late 1970s. That analysis is shown in the first column of Table 3.2. This snapshot deceptively indicates that the rich got richer, the poor got poorer, and the middle class stood still.

But Mr. Burkhauser finds that when making proper adjustments, the income gains were widely shared by every income group. What he found was that just examining the standard Census Bureau income data neglects to account for many factors that equalize income in America today. He made a series of adjustments to that data based on factors such as changes in average family size, taxes paid, government benefits received, and total compensation to workers (not just salary, as explained above). *Every* income group did a whole lot better

Table 3.2: Shared Prosperity and Income Growth, 1979–2007

Shared Prosperity	% Income Growth by Income Group 1979–2007	
	Wages & Salaries	**All Income and Benefits***
Income Quintile	-33%	26%
Poor	-9%	29%
Low Middle Class	2%	37%
Upper Middle Class	12%	40%
Rich	33%	53%
Richest	38%	63%
Median Income	3%	37%

*adjusted for household size, government benefits, taxes, and employer provided benefits

Source: Burkhauser, Larrimore, and Simon, "A Second Opinion on the Economic Health of the Middle Class," National Tax Journal, forthcoming.

during the 1979–2007 period—see the second column of Table 3.2. If we compare the conventional measure of income growth versus the correct measure of how much money these families actually have to spend on a per capita basis, we see much bigger improvement in economic conditions for those in the middle class and at the bottom.

Instead of real median family income rising by a tiny 3.2 percent from 1979–2007 as some scholars have stated (becoming the basis for the common assertion of a middle class running faster and faster on an economic treadmill just to stay in place), with proper adjustments measuring all payments to families, real median incomes and benefits rose by a much more bullish 36.7 percent.

Yes, led by the fabulous innovations and entrepreneurial endeavors of people who became multi-billionaires like Bill Gates and Steve Jobs and Sam Walton, the rich got wealthier at a faster pace over this period with those in the top 5 percent seeing their income rise by 63 percent on average. But even the bottom 40 percent saw gains of 25 percent in income, compensation, and benefits. Professor Burkhauser's conclusion is worth repeating:

> The real income story of the last thirty years in America is not one of stagnation, but one of upward income mobility. The middle class has not shrunk since 1980, a lot of those families simply got richer.

What did this mean for family buying power? The following table breaks down the income gains in actual dollars from 1983–2005. On average, the typical family saw a gain of more than $11,000 in real income and the mean income grew by more than $20,000. Not bad, and certainly a far cry from a decline.

This table confirms the key point that Professor Burkhauser found in his research: Since 1983, every income group has seen an advance in income. It also confirms the gains to the rich were the most impressive.

Table 3.3: After-Tax Real Comprehensive Household Income						
Year	Lowest Quintile	Second Quintile	Middle Quintile	Fourth Quintile	Highest Quintile	All Quintiles
1983	12,500	26,200	38,600	52,700	99,800	45,900
1993	14,000	28,800	42,500	58,500	117,300	52,200
2005	15,300	33,700	50,200	70,300	172,200	67,400
			% Change			
1983-1993	12.00%	9.92%	10.10%	11.01%	17.54%	13.73%
1993-2005	9.29%	17.01%	18.12%	20.17%	46.80%	29.12%

Source: CBO, "Historical Effective Federal Tax Rates: 1979 to 2005."

MEASURING ECONOMIC CONDITIONS OF THE POOR

As the above tables demonstrate, the poor did not realize the same large gains as did the middle class and the rich. Why? One reason that wealthy families have so much more money than families at the bottom is that there are more workers in high than low income

**Figure 3.5: U.S. Distribution of Income in 2002:
Conventional Census Bureau Figures***

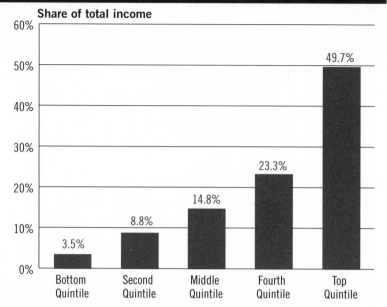

Share of total income

Source: U.S. Bureau of the Census, Current Population Survey for 2002.
*Note: Stage 1 - Conventional pre-tax money income. Quintiles contain unequal numbers of persons.

families. For example, the average household in the lowest income quintile has only, on average, about one person working half-time. This means that many of these families have no one working and earning a salary at all. (It's hard to have a very impressive income if you don't work.) By contrast, the average high income family has on average two people working—usually a husband and a wife. So it should not be too surprising that the rich have more income, since for every hour worked in a low income family, the members of a high income family work four hours.

Here's another statistic that distorts the income gap. The average poor household consists on average of about one and a half people. This means that a lot of low income households consist of a single person living alone. By contrast, the average high income household has about three people living under the same roof. An income of say, $15,000 a

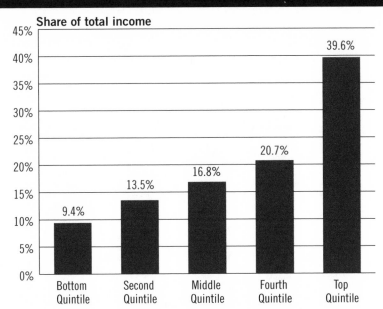

Figure 3.6: U.S. Distribution of Income with Equal Numbers of Persons in Each Quintile*

Source: U.S. Bureau of the Census, Current Population Survey for 2002.
*Note: Stage 3 Figures - Post-tax income including capital gains, health insurance, and non-cash government benefits. Equal numbers of persons in each quintile.

year presents much more a situation of acute financial distress for a family of four than it does for a single person living alone.

So when we adjust for the number of people in the household and the number of workers in the household, we find that at least two-thirds of the income gap "magically" disappears.

Robert Rector of the Heritage Foundation examined the income distribution data in a sample year, 2002. He compared the standard picture that is described by the left with a corrected version, controlling for family size and including all benefits and taxes paid, among other factors. In 2002 the income distribution is obviously tilted to those at the top, but the distribution looks more much more equal than before these adjustments are made. For example, the poorest 20 percent get 3.5 percent of the income before these corrections, but 9.4 percent after the corrections. Instead of the

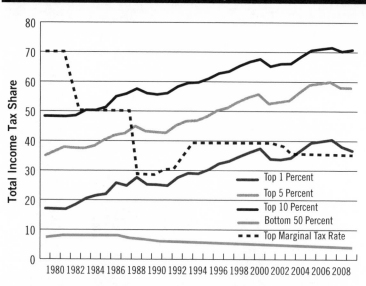

Figure 3.7: Percent of Federal Income Taxes Paid, 1980-2009

Source: *Internal Revenue Service, Statistics on Income, July 2009.*

richest 20 percent corralling about 50 percent of the gains, their share falls to closer to 40 percent.

No, this is not income equality, and it's not clear that is even a goal for most Americans. We like to think of America as a meritocracy: Those who work hard, strive for excellence, take risks, and make wise economic decisions should and must be able to enjoy the fruits of their wise decisions.

There is another statistical trick with the numbers that biases the results in favor of measuring income gains for those at the very top of the income scale. When a poor person over time moves into the middle class or the upper class, that person no longer is classified as poor. So, for example, someone who was earning $20,000 a year and then got a big promotion and saw their income move to $50,000 as they moved up the job ladder, experienced a 150 percent gain in income, but it doesn't count as a gain to the poor because that household no longer is poor. So if a poor person makes $1 million as an athlete or a business owner, we count that person as rich, not as having been poor. But at the same time, every penny of income gain by a rich person is counted because there is no higher income class to move into.

Another problem with comparing the distribution of income from one point in time with another is that about one to one and a half million new immigrants enter the United States every year.[15] A fairly high percentage of these immigrants start at the bottom of the income ladder. This means that America is constantly replenishing the people who are at the bottom rungs of the economic ladder and this naturally makes incomes in America appear to be more unequal than in other nations. This creates the statistical mirage that poor people do not make progress in the American labor force.

THE GAP BETWEEN THE RICH AND POOR

The gap between the rich and poor has been growing, but we need to understand why.

There is no doubt that the share of income going to those at the top rose during the boom period of the economy. According to IRS data, here is how the income shares changed from 1980–2009:

Some of this widening gap is due to statistical measurement changes, such as a definitional revision of "income" in 1986 which meant that more income sources from rich people were counted after this change than before the change. It appears from the Census Bureau data going back many decades that the richest Americans now earn a larger share of the income than at any time since the roaring '20s. It is also true that over the past quarter century the share of income that has gone to the lowest income families—the bottom 20 percent—has fallen from 5.3 percent to 4.1 percent.[16]

But here is a crucial point. The increasingly unequal distribution of income during the era of rapid income growth was because many millions of Americans got unthinkably rich, not because the poor got poorer. Most of the people who got rich in the 1980s and 1990s did not start out rich, but in the middle class or even at a lower starting point.

---

15 U.S. Census Bureau. Foreign-Born Profiles, http://www.census.gov/population/www/socdemo/foreign/datatbls.html.

16 U.S. Census Bureau, Table F-2, http://www.census.gov/hhes/www/income/histinc/f02AR.html.

The real issue in measuring the "fairness" of economic policies and economic results is whether the gains to the super rich have come at the expense of everyone else. That clearly wasn't the case in the 1980s, '90s, and through 2007. As we showed earlier, every income group had a gain. It wouldn't make the poor any better off if the rich lost all their incomes, but by just obsessing over shares of incomes, we would get that impression.

But does anyone really believe that there are Americans who have been made poorer because Bill Gates, Warren Buffett, Tiger Woods, and the members of the Walton family—of Walmart fame— have gotten fabulously wealthy? Clearly not. In fact, each of these people in their own way has not just gotten rich themselves; they have created jobs and higher incomes for many others. It is estimated that Bill Gates alone, whose personal wealth is estimated at $50 billion, is responsible for making over ten thousand people millionaires, including former Microsoft secretaries.[17] The same is true of the people who got in on the ground floor of Google and EBay. When entrepreneurs and investors get rich, they tend to make a lot of other people rich with them. Moreover, nearly every American is a beneficiary of the breakthroughs made by Apple and Microsoft. Walmart has lowered prices for the poorest households in America, and its policy of "everyday low prices" has been one of the most effective anti-poverty programs in history.

The Myth of the Shrinking Middle Class

The big income story of the last three decades has been the upward mobility of the middle class. For the purposes of this section, I define middle class at between the 40th and 60th percentiles in income for families. The Census Bureau tracks what has happened to the incomes of people in this middle category. In 1967 the average income for a middle class family was about $43,000, and in 2007 it was more than $61,000.[18] And this does not include the increased

---

17 Brad Lockwood, *Bill Gates: Profile of a Digital Entrepreneur* New York, Rosen Publishing Group, 2007), p. 60.

18 U.S. Census Bureau, Historical Income Tables – Families, Table F-3, http://www.census.gov/hhes/www/income/histinc/fo3AR.html.

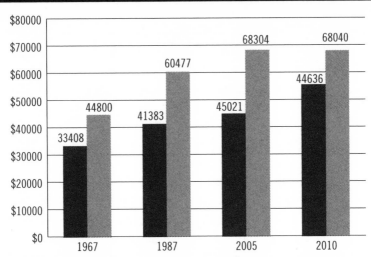

Figure 3.8: Upper and Lower Class Income Limits for Middle Class Families

Source: Household Income, Available at http://www.census.gov/hhes/www/income/index.html

generosity of non-wage and salary benefits like health care, pensions, flexible workweeks, more family leave, more vacation and holidays. These incomes and benefits have, of course, declined since the 2008 recession.

The Census Bureau family income data indicates that:

- In 1967 one in twenty families had an income of $100,000 or more (in today's dollars). In 2005, one in six families did.
- Three times as many families today than in 1967 earn more than $75,000 a year.
- In 1967 the income range for the middle class (defined as the middle 20 percent), ran from $36,600 to $49,000 (in today's dollars). But in 2010 the income range for the middle class runs from $44,636 to $68,040.

That, ladies and gentlemen, is not a *decline* in the middle class.

THE TRENDS IN CONSUMPTION

One way to appreciate the improvement in material well-being of U.S. families today is to examine how Americans spent their money in the past versus now. Anyone who really believes that American families were better off in, say, 1975 than they are today, should engage in this thought experiment: Would you prefer to go back and live in that era?

If you picked the earlier period, this means you have chosen to live without: personal computers, the Internet, cell phones, iPods, GPS systems, DVD players, flatscreen TVs, cable TV, and almost all products and gadgets from the digital age. You would have access to none of the medical technologies, drugs, and vaccines that have come on the market in the past thirty years or so. This means if you were someone like Brian Piccolo (of *Brian's Song* fame), and you got cancer, you were almost certainly given a death sentence—whereas today with most forms of cancer detected at an early stage your chance of survival is well above 50 percent, with the survival rates of some once-deadly cancers well above 80 percent.

If you tore your ACL, your chances of ever running or playing sports again were close to nil. Forget about a hip replacement or modern treatments for back problems. If you had a head injury, forget about having an MRI at the local hospital. Those machines didn't exist. AIDS was a near certain killer in the 1980s; today the death rate has fallen by 80 percent. In 1975 the air was dirtier, water was more polluted, and people lived in more crowded homes, which were much less likely to have air conditioning, or two cars in the garage. Material well-being is not everything, and it doesn't buy happiness, but Americans have a lot more of everything today than in the 1970s.

The big change in the U.S. economy is that not just middle class, but even poor Americans, can generally afford more of so many things that were out of their financial reach a few decades ago.

This isn't to say there aren't poor families really struggling to make ends meet. There are. But the long-term trend is of rising living standards for the poor. Here there is no doubt. Consider, for example, the chart below from my friend Michael Cox at the Dallas Federal Reserve. He shows that the *poor* in America today can afford more goods and services than the middle class could afford thirty-five years ago. It's an amazing story of the wonders of technological advances. What is happening in this age of technology is that new inventions and products are quickly made affordable to nearly everyone. See Table 3.4.

Table 3.4: Everything Is More Affordable: The Ownership Society		
Percent of Households that own:	**All Households, 1970**	**Poor, 2005**
Washing machine	71	72
Clothes Dryer	44	57
Dishwasher	19	37
Refrigerator	83	99
Stove	87	99
Microwave	1	73
Color TV	40	97
Videocassette/DVD	1	78
Personal Computer	1	78
Telephone	93	96
Cell Phone	1	60
Air Conditioner	34	82

Dallas Federal Reserve, based on Census Bureau data

My favorite example is the cell phone. In 1987 a cell phone cost about $4,000 for lousy service, and was a clumsy gadget the size of a brick. Now they are about $39 and they come with cameras, Internet service, calendars, calculators, clocks, and more. The iPhone was first introduced on the market several years ago at a cost of $399. Now that same phone can be purchased for about $150. Soon it will cost less than $100. Now there are "smart phones" that are like miniature robots that cannot only hear your questions, but can talk back to you.

It's not clear that inflation measures entirely account for these massive technological product improvements and such lower costs.

Figure 3.9: The Sears Catalog: 1975 versus 2006

Sears' lowest-priced 10-inch table saw: 52.35 hours of work required in 1975; 7.34 hours of work required in 2006.

Sears' lowest-priced gasoline-powered lawn mower: 13.14 hours of work required in 1975 (to buy a lawn-mower that cuts a 20-inch swathe); 8.56 hours of work required in 2006 (to buy a lawn-mower that cuts a 22-inch swathe. Sears no longer sells a power mower that cuts a swathe smaller than 22 inches.)

Sears' Best freezer: 79 hours of work required in 1975 (to buy a freezer with 22.3 cubic feet of storage capacity); 39.77 hours of work required in 2006 (to buy a freezer with 24.9 cubic feet of storage capacity; this size freezer is the closest size available today to that of Sears Best in 1975.)

Sears' Best side-by-side fridge-freezer: 139.62 hours of work required in 1975 (to buy a fridge with 22.1 cubic feet of storage capacity); 79.56 hours of work required in 2006 (to buy a comparable fridge with 22.0 cubic feet of storage capacity.)

Sears' lowest-priced answering machine: 20.43 hours of work required in 1975; 1.1 hours of work required in 2006.

A ½-horsepower garbage disposer: 20.52 hours of work required in 1975; 4.59 hours of work required in 2006.

Sears' lowest-priced garage-door opener: 20.1 hours of work required in 1975 (to buy a ¼-horsepower opener); 8.57 hours of work required in 2006 (to buy a ½-horsepower opener; Sears no longer sells garage-door openers with less than ½-horsepower.)

Sears' highest-priced work boots: 11.49 hours of work required in 1975; 8.26 hours of work required in 2006.

One gallon of Sears' Best interior latex paint: 2.4 hours of work required in 1975; 1.84 hours of work required in 2006. (Actually, Sears sells no paint online, so the price I got for a premium gallon of interior latex paint is from Restoration Hardware.)

Sears' Best automobile tire (with specs 165/13, and a treadlife warranty of 40,000 miles) 8.37 hours of work required in 1975; 2.92 hours of work required in 2006—although, the price here is of a Bridgestone tire that I found at another online merchant. Judging from its website, Sears no longer sells tires with specs 165/13 and a 40,000 mile warranty.

There was an interesting experiment done a few years ago by George Mason University economist Don Boudreaux. He compared prices of items in the Sears catalog in 1975 versus 2006 and then adjusted the prices for hours of work required to purchase them. Figure 3.9 shows the results. Everything is cheaper, not more expensive!

Lifestyles of the Rich and Famous

One argument for taxing the rich is that they have so much money, they spend lavishly on luxuries at a time when so many are struggling to pay for the necessities. This is an argument made by economist Robert Frank of Cornell University, author of the book, *The Winner-Take-All Society*. He assumes that the rich purchase luxuries that they don't really need and that this is wasteful of societal resources. He says that consumption taxes on the super rich should approach 100 percent to avoid extravagance and waste. But the spending patterns of the rich are surprisingly frugal. It is certainly true that some people who are fabulously rich do buy $300,000 Ferraris and $50 million yachts, and light up cigars with ten-dollar bills and dine on lobster and champagne every night. But they are the exceptions. Overall consumption is the great equalizer in America. According to calculations by former Labor Department economist, Diana Furchtgott-Roth, who has analyzed Census Bureau data on household spending patterns, the wealthiest fifth of Americans now consume $28,272 a year per person compared to $15,639 for the middle class and $11,247 for the poor. [19] Virginia Senator Jim Webb may be right that corporate CEOs now earn a hundred times more than their employees, but they don't consume anywhere near a hundred times more.

It's a sign of the growing affluence of the poor that the single largest increase in expenditures for low-income households over the past twenty years was for audio and visual entertainment systems, which was up about 120 percent. The poor actually spend less money now than twenty years ago on the basic necessities of food and clothing (until very recently with the price spikes for energy and food) meaning they have more disposable income for other purchases—call it the Walmart effect. About 40 percent of Americans meals are eaten out—which again used to be considered a luxury.

A new study by Christian Broda and John Romalis at the University of Chicago finds that we have been statistically understating income

---

19 Diana Furchtgott-Roth, *Economic Security for Working Families.* Testimony before the House Committee on Education and Labor, January 31, 2007. http://edlabor.house. gov/testimony/013107DianaFurchtgottRothtestimony.pdf.

gains of lower income Americans because they buy a different basket of goods than do the wealthy.[20] The poor spend a big percentage of their income on food, clothing, and other basic consumer items that have been stable or even falling in price. Rich people buy new gadgets and upscale, luxury products that tend to rise, not fall in price. If we were to construct an inflation index for poor people, it would show lower price rises than on products for rich people. And that means we understate the income gains of the poor fairly systematically.

Income Gains of Blacks and Women

Remember the "glass ceiling" that women couldn't crack through and that was holding down their wages and blockading their upward career path? In the last twenty-five years or so the glass shattered. Income gains by women outpaced that of men. So the male-female earnings gap *narrowed* in recent decades—a lot. Women saw more than twice the income gains than men did from 1980–2007.

The racial income gap is also closing. Blacks had slightly higher gains in incomes than did whites. And the group that might have been the *most* disadvantaged if prejudice and sexism were rampant in the boardroom and the workplace would be black women. But Figure 3.10 shows the opposite: Black women made the biggest gains. This is very good news. It means that discrimination based on race and sex is declining when it comes to worker pay and that increasingly, pay scales are based on a person's output and the quality of their work, not the color of their skin or whether she wears a skirt.

Since 1980, the average income of black families rose by 44 percent, Hispanic families by 28 percent, and white families by 38 percent.[21] Funny, but we don't read very often about the closing of the racial income gap.

---

20 Christian Broda and John Romalis, "Inequality and Prices: Does China Benefit the Poor in America?," University of Chicago, 2008.http://faculty.chicagogsb.edu/christian.broda/website/research/unrestricted/Broda_TradeInequality.pdf

21 Census Bureau, Historical Income Tables, Families, Table F-6, http://www.census.gov/hhes/www/income/histinc/incfamdet.html.

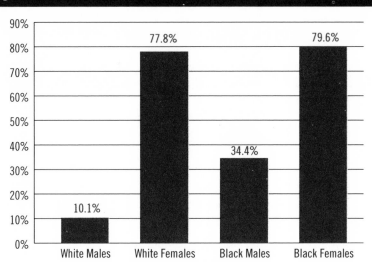

Figure 3.10: Income Gains of Blacks and Women, 1980–2007

Source: Census Bureau. Historical Income Tables, Table P-5

THE GREAT EQUALIZER: INCOME MOBILITY

Until now we have been measuring averages and medians of income categories over time. But people move in and out of these income categories all the time. New immigrants come to the United States and they often start poor but then see their incomes grow. That happens with young people too. When they start in the labor force their beginning salary is low, but as they move from job to job, their income rises. Conversely, some people, such as professional athletes, have a few very high income years but then see a steep decline in their income after their playing days are over.

Income mobility studies examine what happens to real people overtime. These studies allow us to measure how rapidly people move in and out of income categories. The good news is there is a lot of mobility both up and down the income scale. A 2008 study by the Congressional Budget Office found that between 1994 and 2004 the biggest income gains were by those who started the period with the lowest income. The smallest income gains were those who started the period with the highest income. Yes, you read correctly. When you track the income path of real people over time, a Treasury Department study confirmed that in the boom period of the last thirty years, the rich got poorer and the poor got richer. See Table 3.5.

Table 3.5: The Poor Are Getting Richer		
Percent Change in Income		
	1996–2005	**1987–1996**
Poor	109%	81%
Middle Class	26%	9%
Rich	9%	-2%
Super Rich (Top 1%)	-23%	-24%
Super Duper Rich (Top 0.01%)	-65%	n/a

Source: Census Bureau. Historical Income Tables, Table P-5.

A typical poor family that had an income of say, $15,000 a year in 1996, had an income of roughly $31,000 by 2005 (after inflation). Over in Beverly Hills and other wealthy neighborhoods with millionaire households, incomes fell. Many of the super rich in America are people who are celebrities whose talents, fame and mega-earnings years are fleeting. Think of what has happened to the income of Joe Montana, or (the artist formerly known as) Prince, or Kareem Abdul-Jabbar. Lady Gaga and top NFL draft pick Andrew Luck better earn all the millions they can, while they can.

Almost no other nation sees as much mobility over such a short period of time as the United States. This is the reason that immigrants come to this nation—because anyone can get ahead.

The Federal Reserve Bank of Dallas looked at the same income data over a slightly longer time period 1975 –1991.[22] It found that an incredible 98 percent of poor households in 1975 were not poor by 1991. Three out of four of the "near poor," which are those at the bottom 20 to 40 percent in family income, climbed into the middle class or higher over this period.

---

22 Federal Reserve Bank of Dallas, *By Our Own Bootstraps*, Annual Report, 1995, http:// www.dallasfed.org/fed/annual/1999p/ar95.pdf.

What Explains Income Mobility?

One explanation for rapid mobility up the income ladder is that age has a lot to do with one's income status. Those in the bottom quintile tend to be younger. Many are in school with scant income because they do little work for pay. This point is documented by Figure 3.11, which shows that with each passing year in the labor force, their income, on average, rises. Milton Friedman taught us about this lifetime cycle of income many decades ago. The Congressional Budget Office, which came to a very similar finding on income mobility, finds that the landmark welfare reform bill of 1996 succeeded in moving families off of public assistance into jobs, and that those families then saw impressive income gains over the next decade.[23] Yes, that is the same welfare reform that Mr. Obama wants to gut.

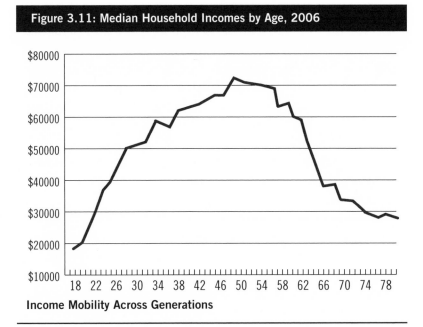

Figure 3.11: Median Household Incomes by Age, 2006

Income Mobility Across Generations

---

23 Congressional Budget Office, *Changes in the Economic Resources of Low-Income Households with Children.* May 2007. http://www.cbo.gov/ftpdocs/81xx/doc8113/05-16-Low-Income.pdf.

INCOME MOBILITY ACROSS GENERATIONS

The beloved and just recently deceased actor Sherman Hemsley played the part of George Jefferson in the 1970s sitcom *The Jeffersons*, a black man who got rich and moved his family to a mostly white wealthy neighborhood of New York. The show's theme song was "Movin' on Up," and that has been a theme in America from the time of our founding as a nation. Anyone can get ahead regardless of race, ethnicity, or humble beginnings.

Barack Obama asserts that isn't happening anymore. Since the early 1980s, he says, the rungs of the economic ladder have been sawed off making the upward climb increasingly impossible. He also alleges that a child born into poverty in the years immediately after World War II had a better than 50-50 percent chance of moving into the middle class; and a child born into poverty in 1980 had a 40 percent chance of moving up; but a child born today will have only a 33 percent chance of "making it to the middle class." Meanwhile, the *New York Times* reports that other nations have much more income mobility from one generation to the next than does the United States. They cite research which finds that most Western European and English-speaking nations have higher rates of mobility." The *Times* reports that in the United States 42 percent of those born in the bottom fifth of income stay there as adults. That compares with many other industrial nations where only about one in three or one in four born in the bottom quintile are found there as adults. Are these gloomy portrayals true?

The story here on income mobility across generations in the United States is admittedly mixed. The question is whether a person born poor is likely to be poor when they become an adult, and are children who grow up in rich households much more likely to be rich themselves as adults. In other words, how much does it matter who your parents are in terms of your own success? We would like to think that what matters most is individual initiative and hard work, not one's genes or one's head start in life.

One thing we do know for certain is that today's workers are generally a lot wealthier than their parents were at the same age. A study that Ron Haskins based on Pew Foundation data, for example, found that two of three Americans have higher incomes than their parents at the same age. Even more impressive: when adjusting for family size 81 percent have a higher income than their parents. So it is *not* true that our parents were better off than we are.

But there does seem to be considerable controversy and some distressing news about the ability of low income Americans to escape the bottom rungs of the economic ladder. Most studies now find that roughly 4 of 10 low income children in America have a low income as an adult. If one's probability of being poor was not related to one's parents income, then that ratio would be close to 2 in 10. Even more distressing is that less than 2 of 10 Americans who grow up in a poor household move into the high middle income or high income category. It's getting harder for a poor person to catch the elevator to the penthouse level of the income pyramid, according to the analysis by the *New York Times*.

A new analysis by economist Scott Winship of the Brookings Institution, a left-of-center Washington think tank, has looked at the mobility data and is not so negative about the trends. Mr. Winship, an expert on economic mobility, points to at least six prominent studies on "intergenerational income mobility." That is, research which compares the income status of parents versus their children when they become adults finds "either no change or rising mobility" in recent decades. He also examined data from a national longitudinal survey of children born between 1962 and 1964 and children born between 1980 and 1982 and compared these cohorts' income when they reached the age of twenty-six to twenty-eight with their parents' incomes, and found that "upward mobility from poverty to the middle class rose from 51 percent to 57 percent" over these two periods. He is reluctant to conclude definitively that mobility increased, but he is emphatic that "the data provides absolutely no evidence that economic mobility declined, whereas the president said it has fallen by 10 percentage points."

Even more confounding is Mr. Obama's assertion that only one in three kids born today in poverty will move out of it. That isn't based on any data or any factual measurement, but pure conjecture by researchers. How does anyone know what the income of a child born today will be twenty-five years from now? More to the point, what is the value of such negative speculation? As Mr. Winship puts it, "all the president is doing is reinforcing any doubt among the poor that they can make it if they try." It is like trying to teach a six-year old to ride a bike but telling her in advance all the reasons she will probably fall.

But Mr. Winship does agree that there is a concern about a more permanent underclass in America emerging. "In particular, it's American men who fare worse than their counterparts in other countries." Men in poor households have a hard time escaping into higher income classes. But this does not have to do primarily with economic factors limiting mobility. It is social factors, such as divorce, out of wedlock births, bad neighborhoods, and extremely dysfunctional schools that don't train children to be highly functioning adults. Most experts on the left and right agree that one of the most important steps to take to reduce income inequality and give every American a fair opportunity to succeed is to have school choice so parents can opt out of failing schools. Welfare reform that continues to promote work over the dole is also critical as well as policies that promote intact families.

What We Know About the Super Rich

Is being really rich—a millionaire or billionaire—an elite club that stays wealthy and privileged year after year? Surprisingly, no. A study by the IRS of the four hundred tax returns each year with the highest incomes finds amazing mobility in and out of this group over time (1992–2008).

To make the cut-off for the IRS's top 400 list in 2008 required an income $109.7 million. This group's average income was $270.5 million.

The IRS found that only four of the four hundred (1 percent) made the cut every year. There were 3,672 different taxpayers who made the top 400 list at least once over this seventeen-year period, with over half of them making the list only once or twice over those years. Three-quarters of the individuals who rose to the heights of this top 400 list were there for six years or fewer out of the seventeen-year period. There is no permanent upper class in America.

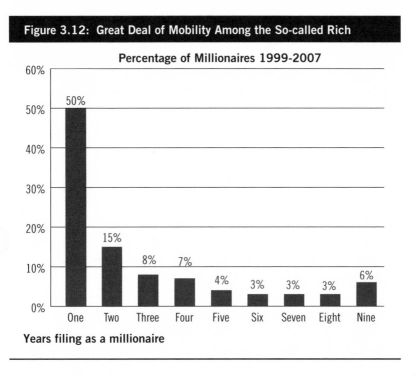

Figure 3.12: Great Deal of Mobility Among the So-called Rich

This data also indicates that it can be very misleading to look at a person's income in just one year because of movement up and down. Many people who show up as "rich" in annual income statistics have sold a lifelong business that was built up over twenty, thirty years or more after pouring a lifetime of sweat equity and family assets into it. Also, it's the natural life cycle of a firm that many businesses suffer years of small profits or even losses before they score a few years of big net profits. This too artificially inflates a few years of very high income that shows up on income tax returns of the "rich." Because of this phenomenon, the IRS used to allow "income averaging" over several years to allow a more reasonable rate of tax paid on one or two years few year of very high earnings.

The point is that "proceeds" from a few years of profits or the one-year sale of a business represent a lifetime of work, but are derided by the left as an ill-begotten windfall that should be taxed at a rate 60 percent higher than today.

This hypothesis is largely confirmed by the IRS statistics. Only 8 percent of the income of the top 400 is from wages and salaries. There just aren't that many A-Rods or Tom Cruises or even CEOs with multi-million dollar annual contracts. The super rich in America are, by and large, owners and operators of businesses and that is how they get their income. For example, 56 percent of their income comes from capital gains, which is often the sale of a family business. Another 20 percent comes from "Partnership and Corporation net income," which is also typically the earnings of a successful entrepreneurial enterprise or a family business.

Increasing those business and capital gains tax rates is likely to extract money from the investor and business entrepreneurial class that play such a major role in job creation. This isn't mostly passive wealth sitting in a vault.

The 2007 Forbes 400 list of the richest people confirms that America remains an opportunity society and that it's not easy to stay on the top rung of the wealth ladder for long. Of the 400 richest people, only thirty-two were there when the list began in 1982.[24] Only 18 percent inherited their whole fortune, while about 70 percent—the people like Jeff Bezos, Michael Dell, Sergey Brin, and Steven Spielberg—amassed fortunes by giving the rest of us products we want. Yes, parentage matters, but individual initiative and achievement matter much more.

EDUCATION AND WEALTH

One of the biggest factors in one's earnings is the quantity and quality of education received as a child. Figure 3.13 shows that incomes are highly dependent on years of education. Those without a high school education have average earnings of $33,419 compared to $58,866 for those with a bachelor's degree and $117,033 for those with a professional degree.[25]

---

24 John Tamny, "The Forbes 400 as a Lesson in Economics," *Real Clear Politics*, September 28, 2007, http://www.realclearpolitics.com/articles/2007/09/the_forbes_400_as_a_lesson_in.html.

25 Census Bureau, Historical Income Tables, Income Level by Educational Attainment, 2010

This doesn't mean that everyone has to go to college. It does mean that a high school diploma is essential and that unless something is done to fix America's dreadful inner city schools, poor children face a hefty disadvantage in the workplace. One thing almost everyone agrees on—those on the left and right—is that in a global economy, returns on education are larger today than ever before.

Figure 3.13: Average Income by Educational Attainment, 2006

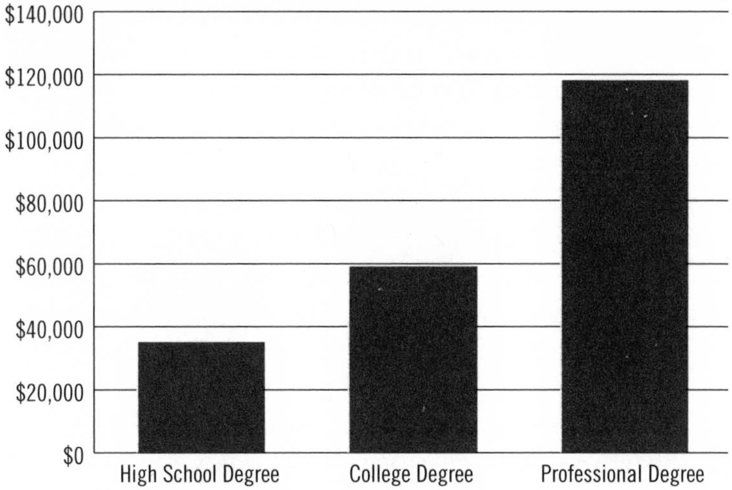

Source: U.S. Census Bureau, 2010

OBAMA: THE INCOME EQUALIZER

Economic growth and progress are not, alas, inevitable. We've learned that during times of prolonged economic distress, such as during the Great Depression, when a cascade of cataclysmic policy mistakes by Herbert Hoover and then Franklin Roosevelt exacerbated a prolonged period of financial misery for families.

We had another lost decade of economic progress in the 1970s. It's striking that Barack Obama keeps saying that the economic demise of the middle class and the poor began in the 1980s. He has that story all wrong. The big declines in real incomes were from 1973–1981: the era of Richard Nixon, Gerald Ford, and worst of all,

Jimmy Carter. The rapid expansion of the welfare state, rampant inflation, and high tax rates doomed the economy to slow and even negative growth. Median family incomes *fell* in the 1970s, but rebounded rapidly in the 1980s after Reaganomics was put in place. A policy change toward the free enterprise system unleashed a wave of growth that benefited all groups.

But now we are again seeing an income decline in America that began with the collapse of the economy in 2008, but has continued for at least the first two years of the Obama presidency and his redistributional policies. By 2011, after Mr. Obama's first three full years in office, and after nearly two years of his radical spending and taxing policies, median American family incomes *declined* by almost $4,500 for every race. The poverty rate rose, and so did the number of Americans losing their homes. Yes, Mr. Obama inherited an economic mess, but his policies have done little to stop the decline.

Mr. Obama and his big Democratic majorities in Congress passed an arsenal of new spending programs—from Obamacare, to subsidies for green energy, to the biggest expansion of the food stamp and department of Education budgets in history—to name a few. At a cost of more than $1 trillion, this was as radical a government expansion as had been implemented since LBJ launched the Great Society and gave birth to the welfare state.

Perhaps the reason Mr. Obama is throwing this Hail Mary pass of class warfare and blaming George W. Bush, congressional Republicans, bankers, Wall Street executives, oil companies, the Japanese earthquake, and the European financial crisis for America's economic rut, is that three years into his presidency, his own policies have failed. This is not a president who dares run on his own record of $4 trillion of debt in three years, 8.5 percent unemployment for more than thirty straight months, and the most anemic recovery measured in family income and GDP growth since the Great Depression. We are still four million jobs below where we were four years ago.

Here is an even more amazing part of the story. The share of income going to the richest Americans has declined rapidly during this recession and slow recovery—so much for redistribution economics.

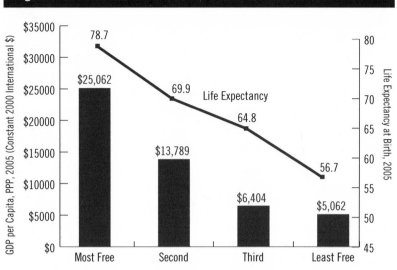

Source: Cato Institute and Fraser Institute, Economic Freedom of the World, 2007.

How Free Markets Create Affluence

Why is it that most of the citizens of the United States are very rich by international standards, but people in Cuba, Zimbabwe, and North Korea are materially very poor? There are lots of explanations but one of the most obvious answers is the free enterprise system. It turns out that the one formula for advancing human welfare, standing head and shoulders above the rest—including all the "isms": communism, socialism, progressivism, Keynesianism, fascism—is economic freedom. This is the magic formula that allows a nation's citizens to advance up the income scale. It is, as Nobel prize economist James Buchanan has put it, "The goose that lays the golden eggs."

Take a look at Figure 3.14. It shows how economic freedom is correlated with economic progress and improvements in health. The freer a nation is, the richer it is. This isn't a complicated relationship. The key to helping the poor and the middle class gain income isn't higher taxes on the rich, bigger government, a welfare state, or more income transfer programs. It is an economic climate conducive to growth—meaning low tax rates, protection of private property rights, a rule of law, free and open trade, and limited government interference in the marketplace.

Freedom = prosperity.

This brings us back to the issue of fairness. Most people accept that the rich and even the middle class do very well under capitalism. But we are told the poor are the ones left behind.

Not so fast. Let us say for a moment that we were going to measure the "fairness" of a society based on the level of income and economic progress achieved by the lowest income group. In other words, we will ignore completely how the top 80 percent achieve and only examine how this society treats the poorest among us.

Surely under that measure more socialist economies based on sharing the wealth are superior. After all, we are told that free enterprise capitalism creates a dog-eat-dog society where the rich win out in a Darwinian model. But that's wrong. My friend Arthur Brooks, the president of the American Enterprise Institute, has just written his own book called *The Road to Freedom,* and it provides

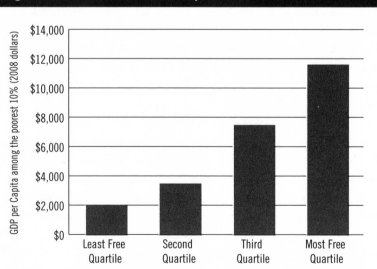

Figure 3.15: Economic Freedom Helps the Poor

Source: James Gwartney, Joshua Hall, and Robert Lawson, Economic Freedom of the World 2010 Annual Report. Fraser Institute.

compelling historical evidence that not only do the middle class and rich do better in free societies (like the United States), but the poor do a lot better too.

The average income of a poor household (the bottom 10 percent) in countries with the least free economies was about $2,000 a year. But in the freest societies, like the United States, the income level of the poor is at least five times higher, or closer to $12,000 a year. Figure 3.15 shows the results: Capitalist societies with more freedom do better for the poor. Which society would you rather be poor in?

To Recap: What Have We Learned?

The left says there have been almost no living standard gains since the 1970s in America. If you believe that, ask yourself this: What if you had your choice between working in the 1970s or working today? Would it have been easier to raise a family, to buy things that you and your loved ones wanted, to get access to first-rate medical care if you got cancer or had a heart attack, or to send your kids to college?

The answer to each of these questions is obviously, no.

Those who say the middle class is no better off today should try living for a week or two without a personal computer, a cell phone, a color TV (much less, cable, or satellite, or HD), the Internet, air conditioning, modern medicines, Walmart, a washing machine, cheap air travel, and so on. For most of us, our kids are our most prized assets. Fifty years ago the death rate for children was twice as high as it is today.[26]

In sum, the average middle class family today has a higher living standard than a rich person in the 1950s when accounting for all the things they can afford to buy that even the rich couldn't get fifty years ago. Your chances of surviving cancer or heart disease are multiple times higher today than in the 1950s. What is that worth? For anyone who is black or a woman, the gains have been extraordinary. In the 1950s most women were still confined to the drudgery of housework. Now women have career options that our grandmothers never would have dreamt of.

---

26 Statistical Abstract of the United States, 2008.

One last point, we started this analysis by asking: Should we divide the pie or grow it? The U.S. model for the past thirty years starting with the Reagan recovery has been to grow the pie so that just about everyone gets a bigger piece—even if some people get a lot more than others. The Western European model (until very recent reforms) has been oriented toward fairness and equity—making sure everyone gets pretty much an equal slice. What has been the result? The United States has created forty million jobs, while Europe, with more people, has created less than half that number. The average purchasing power in the United States today ranks much higher than in almost all European nations. The average U.S. family earns about one dollar for every seventy-five cents earned by the French, Italians, and Germans.

What created the rise in living standards in recent decades was not redistribution, but growth. Mr. Obama claims, "we tried tax cuts and it did not work." It didn't? The supply side tax cuts of the 1980s launched a quarter century of prosperity when the economy was growing more than 90 percent of the time.

Moreover, when the economy was expanding in the 1980s, '90s, and early 2000s, tens of millions of Americans rode up the wealth elevator, rising to higher income strata—including millions of immigrant families (many of whom came to the United States with almost nothing). Families that started poor in 1986 saw income gains of 81 percent over the next ten years. That was a bigger income gain than for any other group. Those who started at the top generally fell out of the top. Mr. Obama is dead wrong when he says that in America those who work hard and play by the rules can't get ahead. They most certainly can—and do.

That is what we call the American Dream.

Chapter 4

Who *Really* Pays
the Taxes in America?

*It is a paradoxical truth that tax rates are too high today,
and tax revenues are too low and the soundest way to raise the revenues
in the long run is to cut the tax rates.... [A]n economy constrained by high
tax rates will never produce enough revenue to balance the budget,
just as it will never create enough jobs or enough profits.*
—John F. Kennedy, 1962, Address to the Economic Club of New York

No issue dominates the political debate around the country more than "tax fairness." We hear it over and over: "The rich don't pay their fair share of taxes." Most of this talk about what group should pay more in taxes is mostly a political diversion from the overspending problem in Washington. The federal budget is now nearly $4 trillion, twice what it was in 2000. The spending disease is what really threatens to paralyze our economic future.

But on taxes, the full court blitz for raising them on the wealthy is making headway. We have a prominent billionaire like Warren Buffett announcing that the tax code "coddles the rich" and that he should pay more taxes. A number of very wealthy Democrats stepped forward and took out newspaper ads to announce that they too pay too little and they *want* to pay more taxes. (Not one of them is on record as simply offering part of his wealth to help pay off the U.S. deficit—the kind of patriotic donation they could make through their 1040 returns.)

What's been missing from this debate are the basic facts about taxes: Who pays and how much?

Getting these tax facts straight is more important now than ever, because we're facing a ticking tax time bomb. Unless the current law is changed, it's going to detonate in January 2013—when the

Bush-era tax cuts and the Alternative Minimum Tax fix all expire.
That means that in 2013, taxes will rise on personal income, capital
gains, dividends, and wages and salaries. Federal taxes are already
scheduled to rise by about $500 billion over the next ten years as a
result of the revenue raisers in the Obamacare bill. Starting in 2013,
investment income taxes will rise, as will taxes on the health care
system and certain health plans. This means we face the largest
tax increase since the end of World War II—which could put future
prosperity in great peril.

Tax Rates and Tax Revenues

President Obama says the people who made the biggest income gains
in America in recent years should shoulder a bigger share of the tax
burden. Mark Zuckerberg, Jamie Dimon, Bill Gates, Albert Pujols,
Katy Perry, and others who have made it big should share their gains
by paying more in taxes. As Mr. Obama puts it, they can afford to pay
more and given their great wealth, who could argue against that?

President Obama hopes to raise $1.9 billion in taxes over the next
decade by raising tax rates on the wealthiest Americans. He wants a
top tax rate of about 42 percent (up from 35 percent today) on anyone
with more than $250,000 in income from salaries, small business
income, and dividends. When you add state and local taxes, many
will face tax rates of up to 50 percent or more.[1]

There's one key problem with this idea. History teaches us that
high tax rates are the worst way to redistribute income to the poor
and the middle class. This is because there is a "Laffer Curve" effect.
Very high tax rates will discourage more work and investment, so the
government may actually get less revenue than if it held rates at a less
confiscatory level. So, for example, a tax rate of 80 percent means the
investor or worker keeps only twenty cents on every dollar earned,
while the government takes eighty cents. The incentive to keep
producing or to continue putting money at risk is stifled. One way to
think about this: If there were a 20 percent tax rate for working on
Monday, a 40 percent tax rate for working on Tuesday, a 60 percent

---

1 Tax Foundation, 2012

tax rate for working on Wednesday, an 80 percent rate for working on Thursday, and a 90 percent rate for working on Friday, how many people would work on Friday? Not many. Rich people also put more of their income in tax shelters and invest more in tax deductible activities when tax rates are high. In other words, the higher the tax rate, the lower the amount of taxable income that shows up on tax returns. Wealthy people have accountants and tax law experts who show them how to avoid paying 50, 60, and 70 percent tax rates.

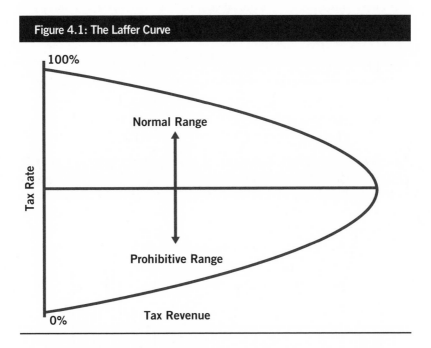

Figure 4.1: The Laffer Curve

We see this Laffer Curve effect from changes in tax rates when we track overall tax revenue collections and the highest income tax rate. Revenues generally don't rise any faster when tax rates are high than when tax rates are low. The economy is what drives tax collections—more people working and more businesses profiting drive up tax revenues. Recessions drive them into the tank. Since high tax rates can slow an economy down by stifling work, savings, and investment, higher tax rates often lower overall tax collections. It is worth noting that lowering one tax—say, the federal income tax rate—often leads to higher tax revenue collections from other tax sources. Payroll tax collections soared in the 1980s as did state and local tax collections with reduced income tax rates under Reagan. Reagan proved that the best way to raise tax revenues is to speed up the economy and put more Americans to work.

The most obvious Laffer Curve effect from changes in tax rates is the capital gains tax—a tax imposed on stock and other asset sales. Investors are highly sensitive to the tax rate. Over the past forty years, every time the capital gains tax rate has been reduced, the revenues from the tax have increased. Every time the tax has been raised, the revenues have fallen. Investors choose not to sell their stocks when the tax rate is high (called a "Lock-In" effect) and are more prone to sell their stocks when the rate is low. So at a high tax rate, the federal government imposes a high rate on almost no income. Mr. Obama wants to double the capital gains tax to 30 percent from 15 percent

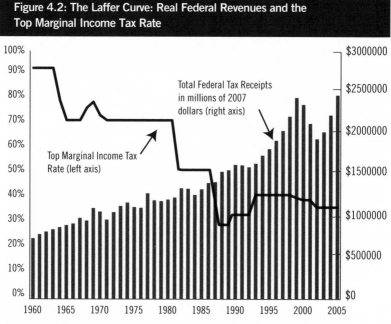

Figure 4.2: The Laffer Curve: Real Federal Revenues and the Top Marginal Income Tax Rate

Source: Office of Management and Budget, Budget of the United States Government, Fiscal Year 2008.

today via the Buffett tax. This is almost certainly going to lose revenue for the government and cause a new Lock-In effect.

TAX RATES AND TAX PAYMENTS BY THE RICH

Imagine you are at an expensive dinner gala with a hundred people in attendance. The cost of the dinner is $10,000, and at the end of the evening it is time to pay the bill. Most would say what is fair is for each of the hundred diners to pay their share of the bill. But now imagine we pay for the dinner the way we pay our federal taxes. In that case, those in the room in the top half of income would pay 97 percent of the tab. Those in the bottom half of income would pay 3 percent. By the way, the forty attendees with the lowest income would pay zero—they eat for free.

Then there are the rich people in the room. The ten richest pay two-thirds of the bill, the three richest pay half, and the wealthiest person of all pays forty percent, or $4,000. Sound fair?

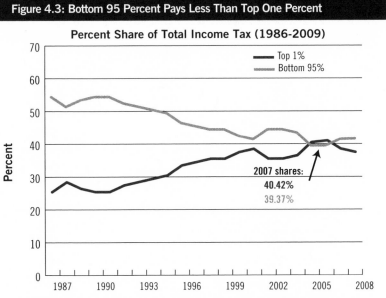

Figure 4.3: Bottom 95 Percent Pays Less Than Top One Percent

Percent Share of Total Income Tax (1986-2009)

2007 shares:
40.42%
39.37%

Source: Internal Revenue Service, Statistics on Income, "Number of Returns, Shares of AGI and Total Income Tax, AGI Floor on Percentiles in Current and Constant Dollars, and Average Tax Rates," Table 1.

Who Really Pays the Taxes in America?

The U.S. tax system is highly progressive in terms of what groups pay the most taxes. The richest 3 percent, roughly those earning more than $250,000 in income, pay a *larger share* of the tax burden than they have since at least 1960. Our government relies for more than 50 percent of its revenue on the richest 3 percent. They are paying more than the other 97 percent combined. Even more amazing, the top 1 percent pay more tax than the bottom 95 percent. It's hard to call that "coddling."

Every year the Treasury Department examines the distribution of federal taxes by income group. The data for all recent years yield the same conclusion: People at the top pay much more than those at the bottom. Let us examine the data for 2007: In that year the richest 1 percent earned 22 percent of the income but paid 40 percent of the income tax. The top 10 percent paid 71 percent of the tab. The bottom 50 percent (those below the median income in America) earned 12 percent of the income and paid just 3 percent of the taxes. It's hard to see how such taxes are "unfair."

Table 4.1: Who Pays How Much in Taxes, 2007

	Share of Income	Share of Federal Income Taxes
Top 1%	22	40
Top 5%	37	61
Top 10%	48	71
Top 25%	68	85
Bottom 50%	12	3

Source: IRS, 2010.

How does the picture change if we include into the analysis *all* federal taxes, not just the federal income tax? "Aha!" reply the critics. "You left out the payroll tax." The Social Security tax is somewhat "regressive" compared to the income tax. Payroll taxes of 15 percent are charged on the first dollar of income earned by a worker, and the tax is capped at an income of just about $105,000. The liberal Tax Policy Center run by the Urban Institute and the Brookings Institution recently studied payroll and income taxes paid by each income group. Here's what they found: The richest 1 percent of Americans still pay a rate of 27.5 percent while the poorest fifth of Americans pay only 4 percent.

Table 4.2: Impact of All Federal Taxes, 2009

Cash Income Percentile	Percent of All Federal Tax	Average Effective Tax Rate
Poor	-0.2	-0.9
Working Class	3.1	6.6
Middle Class	10.5	13.4
Upper Middle Class	19.2	17.2
Wealthiest	67.2	22.9
Top 10 Percent	52	23.9
Top 5 Percent	40.3	24.8
Top 1 Percent	22.9	26.1
Top 0.1 Percent	10.8	27.9

Source: Tax Policy Center, Table T09-0358 and T09-0357

That's because working people in this category get part of their payroll taxes *refunded* through the Earned Income Tax Credit—a fairly efficient program for helping working families. So no matter how you slice it or dice it, the rich pay the bulk of the federal taxes in America.

Now let's examine whether raising the top tax rate on the rich is an effective way to get more tax revenues for the government. We'll examine what has happened to the tax share paid by the richest 1 percent, 5 percent, 10 percent, and 25 percent of taxpayers when tax rates went up, and when they went down from the 1970s through today.

Back in the late 1970s the highest income tax rate was 70 percent. Reagan slashed the top tax rate to 50 percent, and then down to 28 percent in 1986. As we noted above, even though the tax rate fell by more than half, total tax receipts in the 1980s *doubled* from $517 billion in 1981 to $1,030 billion in 1990. That's because the economy grew so much faster and the distribution of taxes became more heavily imposed on the wealthiest tax filers. Since the late 1970s, even as tax rates fell by half, the amount and percentage of taxes paid by the wealthy *vastly increased*.

Table 4.3: Share of Taxes Paid					
	Top Tax Rate	Top 1%	Top 5%	Top 10%	Top 25%
1980	70%	19%	37%	49%	73%
2004	35%	36%	56%	68%	84%

When John F. Kennedy was promoting tax rate reductions in 1963, he put it like this: The best way to promote economic growth "is to reduce the burden on private income and the deterrents to private initiative which are imposed by our present tax system—and this administration is pledged to an across-the-board reduction in personal and corporate income tax rates." Kennedy was proven right, as were Reagan and other tax cutters.

Here is a quick recap on what happened to tax payments by the wealthy during the era of lowering tax rates. Over the whole period 1981–2007, each time the tax rates were reduced, tax payments by the rich climbed:

· At a 70 percent rate in 1980, the top 1 percent paid $47 billion in federal taxes. Today, at a 35 percent rate, they pay *more than $400 billion*. Even after adjusting for inflation, that is a nearly 300 percent increase in tax payments by the super rich.
· After the famous Reagan income tax cuts in 1981, the richest 1 percent *doubled* their income tax payments from $50 billion in 1981 to $114 billion by 1988.
· After the 1986 tax reform act, income tax payments by the rich rose from $70 billion to $146 billion by 1993. Even the congressional budget office finds the rich paid a larger percent of taxes when the rates were lowered.
· After the 2003 tax rate cuts, payments by the rich increased from $256 billion in 2003 to $451 billion in 2007. (The housing bubble inflated some of those revenue gains, also, but there was certainly no revenue loss.)

THE BUSH TAX CUTS AND REVENUES

We're facing a huge, automatic, rise in tax rates unless we do something before January 2013, when the Bush tax cuts expire. Democrats want to raise taxes for those earning more than $250,000—the bulk of America's investors and entrepreneurs— while Republicans want to keep all the lower tax rates in place. It's important that we understand those tax cuts, and what they accomplished for our economy. First, let's remind ourselves what they were. The Bush tax cuts passed Congress in May 2003. The major changes in tax rates were as follows:

- The dividend tax was cut from 39.6 to 15 percent.
- The capital gains tax cut from 20 to 15 percent.
- The personal income tax (highest rate) fell from 39.6 to 35 percent, while the lowest tax rate fell from 15 percent to 10 percent.

We saw more investment, more hiring by businesses, a stronger stock market and other favorable reactions to the lower tax rates from 2003–2007. And here is the kicker: The rich still *paid a higher share* of the tax burden than they had before. In part this was because lower tax rates reduce the incentive for tax avoidance schemes and wasteful shelters, and so raised the amount of taxable income.

4.4: Four Years of Tax Revenue Growth, Clinton Tax Increase Versus Bush Tax Cut Plus Forty Year Average	
Billions of 2009 Dollars	
1993	$1,676
1997	$2,096
Real Revenue Growth	**25.1%**
2003	$2,108
2007	$2,675
Real Revenue Growth	**26.9%**
Average four year real revenue growth, 1970–2009	10.9%

Source: White House Office of Management and Budget, Historical Table 1.3

Amazingly, tax revenues rose more after the Bush tax *cuts* than they did after the Clinton tax *increases*—and the economy grew faster.

Not only did total tax revenues *rise* after the Bush tax cuts, but payments by the rich increased the *fastest*. The total taxes paid by millionaire households more than doubled from 2003–2007, even as the tax *rate* was lowered.

Table 4.6 shows what has happened to the number of Americans who declare more than $1 million in income on their tax returns through 2006. In just three years, there were twice as many millionaires. The best way to get more money from rich people is to *create more rich people*.

Table 4.5: Taxes Paid By the Rich			
Billions of Dollars³			
Adjusted Gross Income			
	2003	**2005**	**2007**
$1 million to $5 million	$78	$123	$155
$5 million to $10 million	$19	$35	$44
$10 million or more	$35	$78	$111
Total $1 million more	$132	$235	$310

Source: Internal Revenue Service, Number of Individual Income Tax Returns, by Size of Adjusted Gross Income, Tax Years 2001–2009

Table 4.6: Tax Returns Reporting Over $1 Million in Income	
2003	181,283
2005	303,817
2007	392,220

Source: Internal Revenue Service, Number of Individual Income Tax Returns, by Size of Adjusted Gross Income, Tax Years 2001–2009

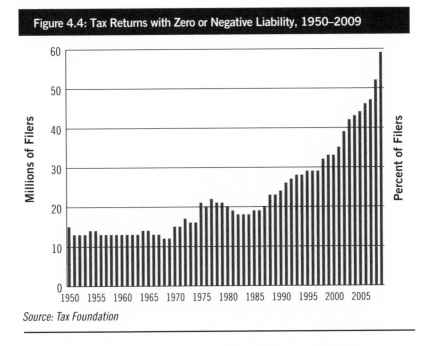

Figure 4.4: Tax Returns with Zero or Negative Liability, 1950–2009

Source: Tax Foundation

Now, of course, the tax payments by the rich (and by everyone) cratered in 2008, and in the succeeding years after the economic meltdown of that year and the Great Recession. But raising the tax rates again isn't likely to be a very effective way to bring in more tax collections.

THE ZERO TAX AMERICANS
Another principle of tax fairness that I believe most Americans would agree with, is that anyone who is a citizen, a worker, and a voter should pay some income tax, even if it is very little, perhaps $100. That isn't the way our tax system works.

That is why when we talk about the progressivity of the federal tax code, we need to examine the burden, not just at the top of the income pyramid, but at the bottom as well. One disturbing trend in the federal tax system is that each year, fewer and fewer Americans pay any income tax at all. The nonpartisan Tax Foundation looked for evidence of tax filers with no tax liabilities and found that in 2008 as many as 47 percent of filers had none. See Figure 4.4.

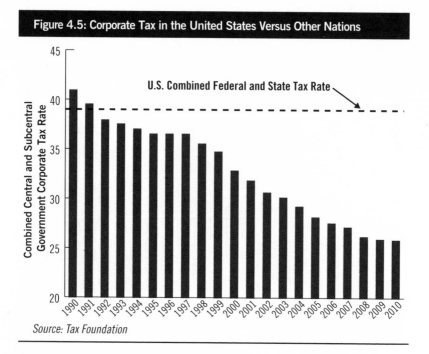

Figure 4.5: Corporate Tax in the United States Versus Other Nations

Source: Tax Foundation

In 2007, before President Obama was even elected, the bottom 40 percent of income earners as a group paid no federal income taxes.[2] Instead, they received net payments from the income tax system equal to 3.8 percent of all federal income taxes.[3] Many of these Americans actually got a check *from* the IRS, because of refundable tax credits, that are like welfare payments. For well more than one of every three Americans, April 15th isn't tax payment day, it's payday from Uncle Sam. Since Mr. Obama was elected president and new "refundable tax credits" have been inserted into the tax code, the problem has only gotten worse. Today, refundable tax credits cost the treasury $81.49 billion a year;[4] these are welfare payments that masquerade as tax cuts.

---

2 Congressional Budget Office, Peter Ferrara, "Federal Income Taxes: Who Pays and How Much, Americans for Tax Reform," Washington, DC, August, 2008.
3 Ibid.
4 Congressional Budget Office, "Refundable Tax Credits: EITC and ACTC." (CRS Report)

TAX FAIRNESS IN THE UNITED STATES AND OTHER INDUSTRIAL NATIONS
Overall, taxes are between 10 and 20 percent lower in the United States
than in most other industrial nations, because we have socialized less of
our economy, than, say, Europe. This gives America more freedom and
a competitive edge in world markets. But America's lead in low tax rates
is shrinking. For example, as of April 1, 2012, the United States now has
the highest corporate income tax in the developed world. Even Obama
administration economists agree that this puts American businesses
and workers at a disadvantage in competing with other nations—as if we
charged a backward tariff on goods going out of the country.

Also, the United States is actually *more* dependent on rich people
to pay taxes than even many of the more socialized economies of
Europe. According to the Tax Foundation, the United States gets 45
percent of its total taxes from the top 10 percent of tax filers, whereas
the international average in industrialized nations is 32 percent.
America's rich carry a larger share of the tax burden than do the rich
in Belgium (25 percent), Germany (31 percent), France (28 percent),
and even Sweden (27 percent).

Table 4.7: Who Taxes the Rich the Most?

	Share of Taxes Paid by Richest 10%
Australia	37%
Canada	36%
France	28%
Germany	31%
Italy	42%
Japan	29%
Sweden	27%
Switzerland	21%
United Kingdom	39%
United States	**45%**
All OECD Nations	32%

Source: Tax Foundation, "No Country Leans on Upper-Income Households as Much as U.S.," 2011.

TAXES AND THE SUPER RICH

Warren Buffett made headlines with his declaration that he pays a lower tax rate than his secretary. But is it true? Many very rich people get their income from capital gains and dividends, which are taxed at a lower rate—because the money is already taxed at the corporate level at 35 percent. The real capital gains tax when taking into account corporate taxes, is closer to 44 percent. Mr. Buffett ignores the corporate tax when he says he pays less than his secretary.

According to the Congressional Budget Office (CBO), in 2009, middle class and low income families (earning $50,000 and below) paid an effective 13 percent of their income in all federal taxes, while those earning more than $2 million paid an average of 32 percent.

HIGH TAX RATES AND SMALL BUSINESSES

Higher income tax rates are an assault on small businesses; the evidence is clear on this point. Most small business owners pay the taxes on their business at the individual income tax rates, according to the Senate Finance Committee. So when tax rates go up on the rich, they go up on small businesses.

Just over half (53 percent) of all flow-through small business income would get hit with the proposal to raise the top tax rate on those making more than $250,000 a year, according to the nonpartisan Joint Committee on Taxation. If we look at the billionaires in the United States, about two-thirds of their income comes from business operations or investments in small businesses. How will we get more jobs when we increase taxes on the businesses that create those jobs? Yes, it is true that only a small portion of the millions of small businesses in America make more than $250,000, but the most successful businesses do make that level of income, and they are the nation's major employers.

Small businesses create 70 percent of new jobs.[5] Higher income taxes are a penalty on hiring more workers. Why would we do that when we have some fifteen million Americans out of work?

---

5 Citation needed: 70% of new jobs small business

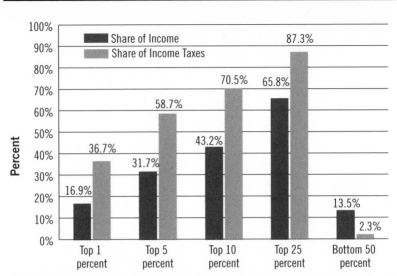

Figure 4.6: The Rich Pay More Than Their Fair Share

Source: Internal Revenue Service, Statistics on Income, "Number of Returns, Shares of AGI and Total Income Tax, AGI Floor on Percentiles in Current and Constant Dollars, and Average Tax Rates," Table 1.

FAIRNESS AND THE OBAMA POLICIES

Because the economy has done so poorly from 2008–2011, tax payments by the rich in this recession have plummeted. According to IRS data, in 2007 there were 390,000 tax filers who reported an adjusted gross income of $1 million or more and paid a total of $309 billion in taxes. In 2009, there were only 237,000 such filers—a decline of 39 percent. Almost four of ten millionaires vanished over two years, and the total taxes they paid in 2009 declined to $178 billion—a drop of 42 percent.[6]

Those with $10 million or more in reported income fell to 8,274 from 18,394 in 2007, a 55 percent drop. Their tax payments tanked by 51 percent as a result.

These disappearing millionaires go a long way toward explaining why federal tax revenues have sunk to 15 percent of GDP

---

6 See table 12, IRS Statistics of Income 2011.

in recent years. The loss of millionaires accounts for at least $130 billion of the higher federal budget deficit in 2009. If Warren Buffett wants to reduce the deficit, he should encourage policies to create more millionaires, not campaign to tax existing ones more.

For the past three decades, the political left has obsessed about income inequality. As the economy experienced one of the largest and lengthiest economic booms in history from 1982–2007, the left moaned that the gains went to yacht club members.

Well, if equality of income is the priority, liberals should be thrilled with the last four years. The recession and weak recovery have been income levelers. Those who make more than $200,000 captured one-quarter of the $7.6 trillion in total income in 2009. In 2007 the over-$200,000 crowd had one-third of reported U.S. taxable income. Those with incomes above $1 million earned 9.5 percent of total income in 2009, down from 16.1 percent in 2007. So we *have* created a more equal society: Everyone is poorer. I fail to see how that is fair.

THE 2013 TAX TIME BOMB

Under current law tax rates are headed way up; and not just on the rich. Even the Alternative Minimum Tax will hit twenty-eight million Americans—with tax bills rising by $2,000 to $3,000 for even people making less than $100,000. Are there really twenty-eight million rich people in America?

Mr. Obama wants that tax time bomb to detonate. Here is what it will mean for U.S. tax rates:

Table 4.9: The Tax Time Bomb		
	Tax Rate Now	**Tax Rate in 2013**
Income Tax	35%	42%
Capital Gains	15%	23.8%
Dividends	15%	43%
Estate Tax	35%	45%

If those tax rates go up, many economists believe it will crash the stock market, contract businesses, and possibly cause a double-dip recession. This economic recovery is too fragile to withstand that punch to the economy's solar plexus (we are still four million jobs short of where we were in 2007). It's never a good time to raise taxes, but it's especially counterproductive to raise taxes when the economy is still struggling to get off its back.

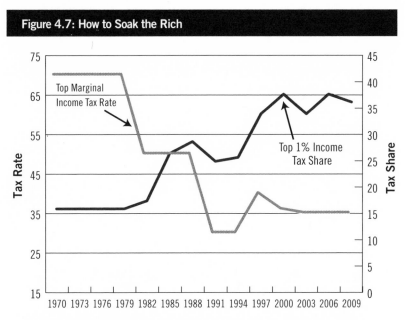

Figure 4.7: How to Soak the Rich

Source: Internal Revenue Service, Statistics on Income, "Number of Returns, Shares of AGI and Total Income Tax, AGI Floor on Percentiles in Current and Constant Dollars, and Average Tax Rates," Table 1.

SUMMING UP

History teaches us over and over that high tax rates are the worst way to redistribute income to the poor and the middle class. And they are the worst way to grow the economy so everyone has a job with a decent salary and at least a middle class income. Closing tax loopholes and sweetheart deals always makes sense. What doesn't is to impose tax policies that reduce incentives to save, invest, and start businesses. I recently reviewed IRS tax return data by income group going back to 1972. The results are jaw-dropping. In 1972, when the highest tax rate on the rich was 70 percent and the top capital gains tax rate was 35 percent, the richest 1 percent of Americans carried 17 percent of the income tax burden. Today, with a top income tax rate of 35 percent and capital gains at 15 percent, they pay 39 percent. [7] With higher income tax rates the rich shelter more of their income through tax carve-outs, they invest less here in the United States and more abroad, and they work less. The Robin Hood strategy has almost always failed because it means less, not more income to take from the rich and give to the poor.

What does it all mean? When politicians put "tax fairness" ahead of economic growth, you produce neither and to no one's benefit.

---

[7] Internal Revenue Service, Statistics of Income, Table 1.

CHAPTER 5

IS A 76 PERCENT TAX RATE
IN AMERICA'S FUTURE?

You'd have to go back to the era of disco music and bell bottom jeans to find the last time politicians and scholars dared to defend tax rates of 70 percent or more, but suddenly that old policy of yesteryear is the retro liberal fashion. It's not enough to resurrect Clinton-era tax rates. We are now told we need to return to Jimmy Carter or FDR levels—this will make for a fairer distribution of the nation's income.

One true believer in this doctrine is Barack Obama. In selling his Warren Buffett millionaire tax, Mr. Obama blasts the failures of "trickle-down economics" and points to a much-cited study by economists Peter Diamond of MIT and Emmanuel Saez of University of California, Berkeley, who argue that raising tax rates to more than 76 percent won't lose revenue for the government or slow down the economy.

Since these two have become the causes célèbres of the new left consensus on raising tax rates, it is worth citing their research and recommendations in some detail. Here is what they argue in an article "The Case for Progressive Tax," in the *Journal of Economic Perspectives* in 2011:

> *The share of total income going to the top 1% of income earners (those with annual income above $400,000 has increased dramatically from 9% percent in 1970 to 23.5% in 2007, the highest level recorded since 1928 and much higher than in European countries and Japan today.*

Allow me to interject here that it is curious that they use 2007 as the ending point, because the 2009 IRS data indicate that the share of income to the richest 1 percent fell very dramatically as a result of the recession. The share going to the top 1 percent is now less than 20 percent, still high, but not nearly a record since 1928.

The authors continue:

> *The taxation of very high earners is a very central aspect of the tax policy debate not only for equity reasons but also for raising revenue. Setting aside behavioral responses for a moment, increasing the average income tax rate on the top percentile from 22.4% to 29.4% would raise revenue by 1 percentage point of GDP. Indeed, even increasing the average federal income tax rate on the top 1% to 43.5%, which would be sufficient to raise revenue by 3 percentage points of GDP, would still leave the after-tax income share of the top percentile more than twice as high as in 1970.*

Again I need to interrupt. One of the central messages of this book is that raising tax rates on the rich will *lower* the share of the taxes paid by the richest 1 percent, as we learned in the 1980s, '90s, and 2000s. The tax rate fell by half over that period, but the share of the taxes paid by the rich doubled.

A study by Martin Feldstein of Harvard, for example, examined real tax returns of four thousand tax filers filed after the 1986 Tax Reform Act, which lowered the highest income tax rate to 28 percent from 50 percent, and found that: "the actual experience after 1986 shows an enormous rise in the taxes paid, particularly by those who experienced the greatest reductions in marginal tax rates." He also found that the incentive effects to work and invest and take risks from the lower tax rates after 1986 instead of investing in tax shelters, meant that the taxable income of the rich increased by 45 percent from 1985-1988. The share of individual income tax liability for the top 1 percent grew to 26.6 percent from 21.2 percent before the rate cuts. Lower rates meant *more* revenues from the rich.

But Professors Saez and Diamond do not see the world that way. They conclude:

> *The optimal tax rate using the current taxable income base...*
> *would be 54%, while the optimal tax rate using a broader income tax*
> *base with no deductions would be 80%.*

That may sound like an astounding conclusion, but they aren't alone. Mr. Obama's first chief economic guru Christina Romer—who predicted that the stimulus would keep the jobless rate below 8 percent—also vouchsafed recently that tax rates can go much higher without harming growth. Not only are high taxes virtuous—they are also a free lunch generating lots of revenues for the government with little economic damage.

The *New York Times* has also hopped on the bandwagon for raising tax rates on the rich. In a 2012 news analysis, the *Times* reports the new left thinking on taxes, so I quote at length:

> *It is true that high-income Americans carry the biggest tax burden.*
> *While fewer than 1 in 20 families make more than $200,000, they pay*
> *almost half of all federal taxes.*
>
> *However they feel about the tax man, there is a case to be made*
> *that they can pay much more. The reason has nothing to do with*
> *fairness, justice or ideology. It is about economics and math.*
>
> *The math is easy: the federal budget over the next decade cannot*
> *be made to square without raising a lot more money. The nonpartisan*
> *Congressional Budget Office estimates that if we stay on our current*
> *path, federal debt held by the public will grow from about two-thirds*
> *of gross domestic product today to roughly 100 percent in a decade and*
> *twice that much by 2040. It is unlikely that even the most committed*
> *Republicans could reverse the trend without higher taxes.*

The *Times* then contends the tax rates don't matter because during the Clinton administration, "taxes rose and the economy surged. It survived George W. Bush's administration, when taxes were cut yet growth sagged." Just the opposite is true, as we showed earlier.

The *New York Times* then contends that "a growing body of research suggests" that "top tax rates could go as high as 80 percent or more."

These high tax rates wouldn't hurt the economy because, "while the rich would respond to a big tax increase by shielding income from the tax man and maybe working less, this would not slow the economy at all. That's because a lot of what the rich do does not, in fact, generate economic growth. So if they reduced their effort in response to higher taxes, the economy wouldn't suffer."

And finally, raising tax rates on the top 1 percent to 67 percent "would raise about $4 trillion over a decade. That's a start."

The point of this book obviously is to educate readers that nearly every word of this *New York Times* piece (which was a news analysis, not an editorial!) is demonstrably wrong.

Even worse, this shatters a policy consensus since the 1980s that low tax rates do the least damage and cause the fewest economic distortions. The Reagan tax cutting experiment inspired a near-unprecedented burst of economic prosperity—an expansion many critics said would never happen. The personal and corporate income and capital gains rate cuts from 70 percent to 50 percent and then to 28 percent from 1981 to 1987 helped create an American renaissance with more than thirty-five million new jobs, some $40 trillion of new net wealth, and a tripling of U.S. output by the year 2000 (to $9.8 in 2000 from $3.1 trillion in 1979).

In Washington, the economic windfall from lowering tax rates was so universally accepted that in 1986 by a vote of 97-3, the U.S. Senate approved a tax reform bill, spearheaded in part by prominent Democrats like Bill Bradley of New Jersey and Dan Rostenkowski of Illinois that chopped the highest federal income tax rate to 28 percent.

Further evidence of the power of this idea came from every corner of the globe as nearly all industrialized nations began to chop their own individual and corporate tax rates to gain competitiveness.

This lesson starts with the recognition that taxes are a toll on economic activity and the higher the rate the greater the discouragement of that activity. As Adam Smith taught us back 1776: If you tax something, you get less of it. We tax cigarettes because we want people to smoke less. We generally tax saving at lower rates, because we want incentives for thrift.

As rates climb higher, their punitive effect is compounded. They create a "wedge" between what a worker costs an employer and what the worker takes home in pay, which reduces both the demand for and supply of labor. When taxing work or investment at a tax rate of, say, 40 percent, the worker keeps sixty cents for every dollar earned. Raise the rate to 70 percent and the after-tax return on work and risk-taking plummets to thirty cents on the dollar.

We learned from a previous chapter that there is at some point a Laffer Curve effect where tax rates get so high, they not only discourage economic activity, they raise less money for the government, because so much activity gets shut down. If someone doesn't work at all, or a business doesn't earn a profit, it doesn't matter how high the rate goes, the revenues are zero. We saw this famously in 1993 when Democrats raised the luxury tax on yachts to get more money from the rich. The tax didn't raise money, it put yacht builders out of business and a lot of middle class workers were the big losers. Congress finally repealed the tax before it did more economic damage.

So what does the academic evidence tell us about tax rates and growth? One study in the prestigious *American Economic Review* by Nobel-prize winning economist Edward Prescott found that Europeans work about one-third fewer hours than workers in many other industrialized nations, and that taxes were a big reason why. In Canada, the United States, and Japan "taxes are lower at the margin," or about 40 percent; whereas rates in France, Germany, and Italy were closer to 60 percent.

He concluded that "virtually all of the large difference in labor supply between France and the United States is due to the difference in tax systems"—that is, U.S. rates are lower. His advice back then is more pertinent than ever, given the financial meltdown across the Atlantic: "Free European workers from their tax bondage and you will see an increase in gross domestic product. . . . The same holds true for Americans." That was advice given more than a decade ago, but the Europeans never followed it.

In a separate study for the National Bureau of Economic Research, Mr. Prescott quantified this relationship between tax rates and work effort:

> *Americans now work 50 percent more than do Germans, French and Italians. This was not the case in the early 1970s...this marginal tax rate accounts for the predominance of the differences at points in time and the large change in relative labor supply over time.*
>
> *Regressions on rich-country samples in the mid 1990s indicate that a unit standard deviation tax rate difference of 12.8 percentage points leads to 122 fewer market work hours per adult per year, a drop of 4.9 percentage points in the employment-population ratio, and a rise in the shadow economy equal to 3.8 percent of GDP.*

In a 2000 study, former Congressional Budget Office director Douglas Holtz-Eakin and former Treasury Department economist Robert Carroll examined the behavior of entrepreneurial businesses and found that "increases in marginal tax rates strongly affect the growth, hiring and survival of those enterprises." Mr. Holtz-Eakin recently examined the tax returns of those in the highest two tax brackets scheduled to rise next year under the Obama plan. He found that about $500 billion, or just under half, of the $1 trillion of small business income reported on individual tax returns will be subject to the higher tax rates. His study estimates those taxes could cost nearly three million jobs and reduce small business hiring by 18 percent.

The level of investment is even more sensitive to the tax rate on income and capital gains. The higher the tax on investment, the lower the rate of return (after-tax). Thus, fewer projects or enterprises get started. This is called the tax "hurdle rate" of investment. The harmful effect of investment taxes is compounded in recent decades because of globalization. When the United States raises its capital gains and individual income tax rates, the comparative benefit of sending money overseas is enhanced.

In the 1970s, for example, when tax rates hit 70 percent, the United States was a net exporter of capital, as investment flowed overseas. After 1981 when personal income tax rates fell to 50 percent and then 28 percent from 70 percent, foreign investment in the United States skyrocketed. That surge in capital investment into the United States happened again after Bill Clinton signed off on a capital gains tax cut in 1997 and George W. Bush did the same in 2003.

History teaches us that in some cases (certainly not all) lower tax rates can increase overall revenues and raising rates can cost revenues (the Laffer Curve effect). Revenues went way up when President Kennedy cut the highest federal tax rate to 70 percent from 91 percent and helped create budget surpluses by the late 1960s. Federal revenues also doubled after President Reagan cut the highest rate to 28 percent from 70 percent. As we saw earlier, revenues have tended to grow at a steady pace even when tax rates were lowered.

Professors Saez and Diamond argue that tax rates of 70 percent or more can raise a lot of revenues as long as Congress eliminates loopholes so that high income earners won't be able to shield their income from taxes as they did in the 1950s, '60s, and '70s.

This is the ultimate in political naïveté. Have these two scholars even been to Washington? High tax rates create the lobbying frenzy for tax shelters. Even the left's moral case for high tax rates—to redistribute income from rich to poor—is undercut by real world evidence. Over the last forty years lower tax rates have been associated with a higher share of taxes paid by the rich, the opposite of what Democrats claim their policies will achieve. When income tax rates hit 70 percent the richest 1 percent paid 19 percent of all income taxes; with a 35 percent rate, they pay about double that amount. Maybe Mr. Obama should try cutting the rates if he wants millionaires to pay more.

Professors Saez and Diamond and Romer counter that the U.S. economy performed well in the 1950s and 1960s with tax rates as high as 91 percent, so we can return to those levels with economic impunity. But today it is much easier to move investment across international borders. Fifty years ago most countries had tax rates that rivaled those of the United States—so there were fewer places of tax sanctuary. China, India, and Brazil were economic backwaters and no threats at all. We were almost literally the only game in town. Today

American workers and manufacturers are in cut-throat competition with those economic gazelles.

Finally, the biggest boom in that era was in the mid-1960s, after the Kennedy rate cuts that slashed the highest tax rate to 70 percent from 91 percent. This tripled after-tax returns from work and investment from 9 percent to 30 percent, and right on cue taxes paid by the rich soared over the next four years. But in the longer term even a 70 percent tax rate was unsustainable. Saez, Diamond, and Romer may want to explain why in those salad days when the tax rate was 70 percent in the late 1960s and 1970s, stocks in real terms lost more than 67 percent of their value.

A landmark study by Nobel-prize winning economist Robert Lucas, presented as his presidential address to the American Economic Association in 2003, compared over fifty years the effectiveness of short term Keynesian interventions into the economy (like the Obama $800 billion stimulus) with what he called "supply side economics" policies reducing tax rates. He concluded that "the potential gains" of the Keynesian approach are "perhaps two orders of magnitude smaller than the potential benefits of available 'supply-side' fiscal reforms." Professor Lucas (who was not originally persuaded by the arguments for lower tax rates in the 1970s when Jack Kemp, Ronald Reagan, Arthur Laffer, and the editors of these pages were making them) now argues that tax rate reductions delivered such irrefutable economic benefits that they were "the largest genuine free lunch I have seen in 25 years in the business." With the U.S. economy still flat on its back, a free lunch sounds awfully good right now.

Gains and Losses

The capital gains tax collections are particularly sensitive to the tax rate and this is therefore one of the most counterproductive ways to raise taxes on the rich. Mr. Obama's plan would raise the capital gains rate on January 1, 2013 to 20 percent on those who earn more than $200,000 ($250,000 for couples) plus add on 3.8 percent investment surtax from the Obamacare law. That 23.8 percent rate is up almost 60 percent from the 15 percent rate that has been in effect since 2003.

Figure 5.1: Capital Gains: Lower Tax, More Revenues (since 1977)

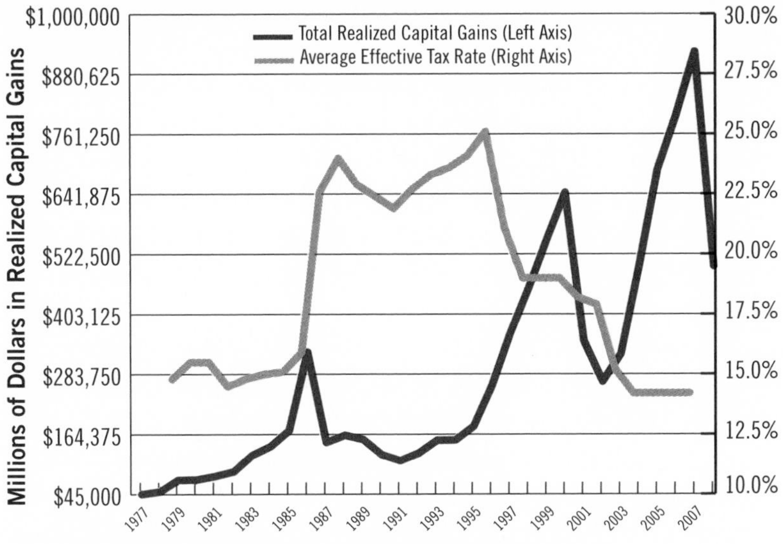

Source: http://www.treasury.gov/resource-center/tax-policy/Documents/
OTP-CG-Taxes-Paid-Pos-CG-1954-2008-12-2010.pdf

The so-called Buffett tax which creates a minimum tax rate of 30 percent on those who earn more than $1 million a year would create a 30 percent tax on capital gains.

There are a lot of reasons this genuflect to the altar of tax fairness is ill advised, not least of which is that it won't raise any money for the government, even though the feds think that billions will flow into the treasury. Not likely.

Ever since the famous 1978 bipartisan capital gains tax cut to 28 percent from 35 percent sponsored by the late William Steiger, one result has been observed over and over: Raising the capital gains rate reduces revenues and lowering the rate has always increased revenues. That seems counterintuitive, but the Figure 5.1 shows it to be true.

After the 1978 20 percent rate cut, the capital gains revenues rose to $11 billion in 1980 from $7.7 billion in 1977.

In the early 1980s when Ronald Reagan cut the rate again to 20 percent from 28 percent, revenues doubled to $23.7 billion in 1984 from $11 billion in 1980.

In 1986 when the tax rate was headed back up to 28 percent there was a huge sell-off of stocks before the tax hike, then a collapse in revenues after the higher rate went into effect in 1987. But then revenues collapsed by more than half from 1986 to 1990.

In 1997 Bill Clinton and the Republicans cut the rate back down to 20 percent and revenues rose by more than 50 percent, to $127 billion from $79 billion.

Then in 2003 George W. Bush and the Republicans chopped the rate to 15 percent and even at that low rate revenues more than doubled to $110 billion in 2006 from $49 billion in 2002. A 25 percent rate cut led to a 130 percent increase in the tax collections.

In each of these cases there was a clear Laffer Curve effect—lower rates meant more revenues. That was predictable for several reasons. One is that the capital gains tax is an elective tax imposed on the owners of stocks and other assets. Investors can avoid paying the tax by locking in their gains and not selling their stock until the tax rate goes lower. So the higher rates generate disappearing gains for the government to tax. This "Lock-In effect" of high capital gains taxes is economically inefficient because it freezes capital into older companies with lower growth potential and away from new ventures with higher returns.

But the most important reason to oppose a higher capital gains tax is that it will hurt workers and the economy. A lower capital gains cut also makes ownership equity more valuable (because of the higher after-tax returns) so there is more appreciation in stock values (that is, "gains") when the tax rate is lower. This problem is going to be compounded in 2013 because at the same time Mr. Obama wants to raise capital gains taxes, he wants to nearly triple the other tax on stock ownership, for dividend income. This will only make stock values lower still and thus further reduce gains from sales of stocks.

With capital markets now paralyzed by fear and investors stampeding away from risk to the safety of government bonds, it would be hard to imagine a worse time to raise the tax on capital investment. It was none other than liberal economic icon John Maynard Keynes who wrote that "the weakness of the inducement to invest has been at all times the key to the economic problem." That's as true today as it was in the 1930s.

Democrats' obsession with raising the capital gains tax comes from a mistaken belief that the preferential rate applied to the sale of a family business, farm, or financial asset is a "loophole" which advantages mostly rich plutocrats. Leonard Burman, a tax professor at Syracuse University, has advised Democrats: "If you want to tax the rich, a really effective way to do it is to tax capital gains." And they're listening.

They're also ignoring the vital linkage between capital gains tax rates and capital investment in new and expanding businesses—the lower the tax, the greater the incentive to take risks. And though Warren Buffett may not believe that tax rates matter, studies by economists such as James Poterba of MIT have documented the "significant influence" of capital gains taxes on the "demand for venture funds."

Thanks to a series of reductions in the capital gains tax rate in 1978, 1981, 1997, and 2003 (the tax was raised in 1986, see Figure 5.1) the capital gains tax has fallen from 40 percent to 15 percent. These rate cuts incentivized investing and unleashed hundreds of billions of venture capital funding and "angel investment" which injected the first or second round of incubator capital into business start-ups. These funds helped launch America's entrepreneurial and high tech revolution over the last thirty years, exemplified by iconic American firms ranging from Google to Walmart to Microsoft to Home Depot, that today employ hundreds of thousands of Americans—think of Peter Thiel's early stage investment in Facebook, as made famous in the movie *The Social Network*.

It's easy to observe these wildly successful ventures and think that investors had a license to make easy money and then they got to pay bargain tax rates to boot. (Why didn't we all have the good sense to do what Peter Thiel did?) But those jackpot pay-offs are the rare exceptions. The returns from the entrepreneurial ventures with big profits have to compensate for the investments that go belly-up. About two of three small businesses fail and investors in these cases incur losses not gains. The indispensable role of Wall Street and private equity firms like Bain Capital is to allocate capital to the firms that are most likely to succeed.

Far from being a loophole, the low tax rate applied to capital gains is beneficial and "fair" for several reasons. First, under the current tax rules, all gains from investments are fully taxed, but all losses are not fully deductible. This asymmetry is a disincentive to take risks.

Second, capital gains are not adjusted for inflation, so a dollar invested in an enterprise over a long period of time, since, say, the 1980s, is partly real gain and partly an inflationary gain. Because the appreciation in stock or a business's value is not indexed for inflation, it's possible for investors to pay a tax on "gains" that are purely illusory, which has been one of the reasons for the lower tax rate.

Third, since we tax corporations and businesses on their profits when they are earned, the tax on the sale of a stock or a business is a double tax on the income of a business. When you buy a stock its valuation is the discounted present value of the earnings. But the company's profits are also taxed in the year they are made. Many economists believe that the economically optimal tax on capital gains is zero. Barack Obama's first chief economic advisor, Larry Summers, wrote in the *American Economic Review* in 1981 that elimination of capital income taxation would have "very substantial economic effects" and "might raise steady-state output by as much as 18 percent." (Maybe that is why he now suggests that the 2013 tax hike should be suspended.)

Finally, we tax capital investment at low rates because we want to encourage greater levels of saving and investment. If someone takes their money and buys a car or a yacht or a vacation, they don't pay any extra federal income tax. But if they save those dollars and invest them in the family business or in stock, wham! They are smacked with another round of taxes.

Almost all economists agree (or at least used to agree) that keeping tax rates low on investment is critical to economic growth, rising wage rates, and job creation. Robert Lucas estimates that if the United States eliminated its capital gains and dividend taxes (which Mr. Obama also wants to increase) the capital stock of plants and equipment in America would be twice as large, which over time would grow the economy by trillions of dollars. Moving in the opposite direction has disastrous effects. Economist Allen Sinai estimates that raising the capital gains rate to between 20 and 28 percent, would reduce U.S. employment by between 231,000 and 602,000 jobs a year and "negatively affects the federal budget deficit."

Even on class warfare grounds, it is counterproductive to raise taxes on capital. Most of the returns to investment in a business benefit workers (not the shareholders), because they become more productive on the job with the modern factories, computers and robotics, and equipment that are made possible with investment capital. This is a point that the late Nobel laureate, Paul Samuelson, and a member of John F. Kennedy's council of economic advisers, made concisely by noting that when a worker has more capital to work with "his or her marginal product [or productivity] rises. Therefore, the competitive real wage rises as workers become worth more to capitalists and meet with spirited bidding up of their market wage rates." Isn't that precisely what we want in America today—a capital investment revival that inspires new business creation and a spirited bidding up of stagnant wage rates as workers produce more? Democrats who argue for higher taxes on capital are in fact advocating slowing down investment and dooming workers to fewer jobs and at lower wages. That isn't fair to anyone.

THE SHAREHOLDER TAX

Nor does it make much sense on fairness or economic grounds to double the tax rate on dividends. If the plan becomes law in January, it would be one of the most damaging assaults on shareholders in recent times. And, sorry, but the biggest victims of the policy wouldn't be the Warren Buffetts and Mitt Romneys of the world, but millions of middle class senior citizens who depend on dividends as a major source of income in their retirement years.

Mr. Obama proposes raising the dividends tax rate to the new higher personal income tax rate of about 41 percent (when counting out phase-outs of deductions). This new rate would apply to those earning more than $250,000. Add to that the 3.8 percent investment tax surcharge in the Obamacare law, and, *voila!* You have a new tax rate of 44.8 percent. Yes, that's just shy of three times the 15 percent rate today. The reason for the reduced tax rate on dividends, of course, is that shareholders only receive these payouts *after* the corporation is hit with the 35 percent corporate tax rate applied to a firm's profits. So with a 35 percent corporate tax and a 44.8 percent dividend tax, the total tax on corporate earnings passed through as dividends would be 64.1 percent for certain "rich" shareholders. That will do wonders for American competitiveness.

Because the new super-dividend tax will only apply to a small fraction of taxpayers, the revenues collected will be a micro-fraction of the $1.3 trillion deficit. But consider the costs. The plan gives new meaning to the term collateral damage, because even though it is directed at the very rich, shareholders of all incomes will share the pain. Here's why: Historical experience indicates that dividend payouts by corporations are highly sensitive to the dividend tax. Dividend payouts fell out of favor in the corporate culture of the 1990s when the dividend tax rate was roughly twice the rate of capital gains. Paying a dividend under that tax policy became what investors called a "non-tax-rational option." When the rate was cut to 15 percent in 2003, dividend payouts of S&P firms surged by 11.3 percent annually, rising to $227 billion in 2006 from $148 billion in 2002, an 11.3 percent annual rise. The federal government collected about a $12 billion a year windfall in extra tax revenue from the higher dividend payouts.

Shortly after the rate cut, Microsoft, which had never paid a dividend, distributed $40 billion of its retained earnings into a massive special dividend of about $3 per share. If Keynesians like cash infusions into the economy, this was one of the biggest stimulus plans in history. In all, there were twenty-two S&P 500 companies that didn't pay dividends before the tax cut that began paying them in 2003 and D04. The list includes Viacom, with a payout of more than $400 million annually, Harrah's Entertainment, Staples, Best Buy, and Reebok. The number of S&P 500 companies paying a dividend reversed a twenty-five-year decline.

If the Obama Treasury Department doesn't think taxes influence corporate behavior, they should review this experience. Or they can listen to former Citigroup CEO Sandy Weill who explained: "The recent change in the tax law levels the playing field between dividends and share repurchases as a means to return capital to shareholders. This substantial increase in our dividend will be part of our effort to reallocate capital to dividends and reduce share repurchases."

Home Depot CEO Bob Nardelli echoed that verdict: "Given the recent changes in the tax law, the increased dividend is an effective way for the company to return capital to shareholders." And that's what happened.

If you reverse the policy, you reverse the outcomes. The tripling of the dividend tax will have a dampening effect on these payments—call it the Obama anti-stimulus—as billions of dollars of dividend checks don't get sent out. Who gets hurt? Recent IRS data finds that retirees and near-retirees who depend on dividend income are frontline victims. Two of three dividend payments go to those over the age of 55, and more than half go to those older than 65. Does Mr. Obama really want to jeopardize the senior citizen vote?

The biggest losers are American shareholders of all incomes. The effect of the higher dividend and capital gains taxes is to make stocks much less valuable. A share of stock is worth the discounted present value of the future earnings stream *after tax*. The higher the tax penalty on owning the stock through dividends and capital gains taxes, the more that the valuation of stocks falls. In the extreme example, if Mr. Obama wanted to raise the dividend tax and capital gains tax to 100 percent, stocks would have zero value and tens of trillions of dollars of wealth would be vaporized. Moreover, if investors become convinced later this year that dividend and capital gains taxes are going way up on January 1, 2013, we are likely to see one of the biggest sell-offs of U.S. securities in modern times to trade ahead of paying these higher rates.

The question is how any of this policy helps anyone. According to the Investment Company Institute about 51 percent of adults own stock, which is more than a hundred million shareholders. Tens of millions more own stocks through pension funds. Why would the White House endorse a policy that will make these households poorer, and potentially tank the stock market? Seldom has there been a clearer example of a redistributionist policy that is supposed to soak the rich that will in fact drench almost all American families.

STATES OF TAXATION

Perhaps the most persuasive evidence on the superiority of low tax rates comes from comparing economic performance and taxes in the fifty states.

I've argued throughout this book that American workers, families, and businesses are repelled by high taxes. Many policymakers and economists (for example, Barack Obama and *New York Times* columnist Paul Krugman) remain unconvinced. We've all heard the arguments: People and businesses don't change their behavior in response to government policy. No matter how high the taxes or how onerous the regulations, we've been told, people will pretty much simply grin and bear it no matter how many weights government places on their shoulders.

But how do they explain a state like Texas? It has no income tax and yet it had almost all of the new jobs from 2005–2010.

Or, consider the 2010 U.S. Census data, which tracks population trends among the fifty states. Those numbers tell us a lot about what states and regions of the nation are prospering, and which are in decline. This new data confirms an unmistakable migration pattern over the past decade: the higher the taxes and the tighter the government choke hold on the state economy, the more likely people are to pack up their bags and leave—or for people outside the state to stay away.

The Census data tells us that over the past thirty years, tens of millions of Americans (and immigrants) have voted with their feet, against anti-growth policies that reduce economic freedom and opportunity in states mostly located in the Northeast and Midwest. The new numbers released from the Census Bureau reveal the full extent to which America has become a nation of movers and shakers (literally). The data shows:

- In a typical year, nearly forty million Americans change their
- home address.
- This means that about one in eight Americans moves each year.
- About one-third of all relocators move across state borders and
  move to a new state they will call home.
- Over the last three decades, there has been a 25 percent increase in
  people residing in a state other than the one they were born in.

The big winners in this interstate competition for jobs and growth have generally been the states in the South and West, such as Texas, Tennessee, Georgia, and Florida. The big losers have been in the rust belt regions of the Midwest. The demoralizing symptoms of economic despair in declining states like Michigan, Ohio, and Illinois, include lost population, falling housing values, a shrinking tax base, business out-migration, capital flight, high unemployment rates, and less money for schools, roads, and aging infrastructure.

But now America's rust belt region which used to be confined mostly to the liberal upper Midwest, extends to virtually every state in the Northeast. With the exception of Delaware, every one of the twenty states north of the Mason-Dixon Line from Minnesota through Maine had below average population growth. The Northeast is looking more like the economically moribund continent of Europe all the time, which isn't a big surprise since the left wants American to emulate Euro-land.

Meanwhile, the booming states in the West and the South have been busy racing to the top, fortifying their economic and political clout over the last decade. Every one of the twelve westernmost states had a population growth above the national average.

The Census migration patterns confirm that at least over the past decade, liberal economic policies based on redistributing wealth rather than creating it, are repelling people and low taxes and limited government are attracting people. The ten states with the highest population gain increased their resident population by 21 percent and had a top tax rate of 4 percent on average, whereas the states with the smallest population gain grew only one-tenth that rapidly, or by 2 percent, and their top tax rate was just under 7 percent. That's a giant difference.

Table 5.1a: Top Winners

	Population Change	Top Income Tax Rate
Nevada	35.10%	0%
Arizona	24.60%	4.50%
Utah	24%	5%
Idaho	21.20%	7.80%
Texas	20.60%	0%
North Carolina	18.50%	7.75%
Georgia	18.30%	6%
Florida	17.60%	0%
Colorado	16.90%	4.63%
South Carolina	15.30%	7%
Average	21.20%	4%

Table 5.1b: Top Losers

	Population Change	Top Income Tax Rate
Michigan	-0.60%	6.85
Rhode Island	0.4	6.50%
Louisiana	1.4	3.90%
Ohio	1.6	7.93%
New York	2.1	12.62%
West Virginia	2.5	6.50%
Vermont	2.8	9.40%
Massachusetts	3.1	5.30%
Illinois	3.3	3.00%
Pennsylvania	3.4	7.05%
Average	2	6.90%

It must be infuriating for "progressives" in states like Connecticut, Massachusetts, New Jersey, and New York to learn that their states are attracting fewer new people than states that they have long ridiculed as backwaters, such as Alabama and Arkansas. Massachusetts, New York, and Rhode Island had less population growth than the nation's poorest state, Mississippi.

But doesn't the nicer weather—rather than tax policy mostly explain these variations? No question, weather matters and milder climate states are definitely doing better as Northeast and Midwest snowbirds have migrated to the South and West. But weather doesn't explain everything. Even if we look within regions of the country we see differences in economic outcomes that weather can't explain. For example, California has long been the jewel of the West Coast, except that it has raised taxes and imposed ever more stringent environmental and workplace regulations. It ranked second to last in population growth of the twelve western most states, ahead of only Montana. Or consider North Dakota and South Dakota. These states are the same in nearly every way and separated only by an arbitrary line that runs through the plains and the wheat fields. North Dakota has a near 5 percent income tax; South Dakota is income tax free. South Dakota grew by 7.9 percent versus North Dakota's 4.7 percent.

Or how about this one: Alaska has possibly the worst climate in the country and Hawaii has arguably the best. But no-income-tax-Alaska had a slightly faster population growth than the state with one of the three highest income tax rates, Hawaii, over the last decade. Amazing, but true.

Here's one explanation for why people and businesses are choosing some states over others. Of the nine states with no income tax, seven had above average population growth, and only two, New Hampshire and South Dakota, were below the average. Nevada, Texas, and Florida, each of which has no income tax, all ranked in the top eight in migration. The other five of the fastest growing states had very low overall tax burdens. New Hampshire's population growth rate was only 6.5 percent, but that was by far the highest in the New England region, and double the rate of growth of its sister state, Vermont, which has one of the highest income taxes. It's not just rich people who are repelled by high taxes.

Beware the Class Warriors

Class warfare is, alas, still a common theme in state capitals just as it is in Washington, and the results of "steal from the rich" thinking are just as unrewarding. At the start of the great recession in 2008 and 2009, tax hikes aimed at the rich were in vogue. Reports the Tax Foundation: "We have rarely seen so many states raise tax rates on the highest income group." The rises in the highest tax brackets were all enacted in states with Democratic-controlled legislatures, reports Stateline.org. In each case, Stateline reports, "Democrats muscled through the tax rate increases, arguing that wealthier residents can afford a higher share of the tax burden—particularly in a recession." In Hawaii, which now has one of the highest state income tax rates (11 percent) in America, Lowell Kalapa, the head of a liberal think tank and one of the lead advocates of the big tax hike on the rich enacted in Honolulu, explained the rationale for the rise by stating: "Working class Hawaiians see millionaires and billionaires buying vacation homes here...so that just drives them to insanity." We wonder whether these working class folks Mr. Kalapa is talking about are feeling better now that these rich millionaires and billionaires have fled Hawaii and the state is in a financial collapse. The tax hike targeted toward these rich people is hardly going to help rebalance the worst real estate crisis in decades in Hawaii.

I doubt the tax hikes aimed at the wealthiest residents are done. In the 1970s, before the tax revolt of 1978 started in California with Proposition 13, some states like Delaware had tax rates as high as 15 percent. It's a good bet that liberal legislatures will continue to try to raise rates on businesses and high-income residents.

I hate to pick on California, New Jersey, and New York, but they continue to be models of how not to govern a state—though Governor Chris Christie is heroically trying to turn things around in New Jersey. These three states each impose tax rates at or near the highest in the nation. They are about twice the national average. Our examination of the data from the state revenue offices discovered that in 2008 these jurisdictions collected between 40 and 50 percent of their income tax revenues from the wealthiest 1 percent of tax filers (see Table 5.2).

Table 5.2: The Terrible Trio		
Share of Taxes Paid by Rich		
	Tax Share Paid by Top 1%	Highest Tax Rate
California	48%	10.55%
New Jersey	46%	10.75%
New York	41%	8.97%

** This is percent paid of those making more than $500,000 a year or the richest 1.3% of tax filers.
Sources: State and city revenue offices; Manhattan Institute; California Tax Commission; and
Tax Foundation*

Guess which three states have about the worst finances today?
California is its own world of ugly and wants to raise its top tax rate to
13 percent. There may not be any rich left to tax.

DOES GOVERNMENT SPENDING CREATE JOBS?
ASK GREECE AND WASHINGTON

This chapter would not be complete without examining the effects
of the alternative liberal model of creating jobs and growth.
Liberals eschew tax cuts and want more government spending
to juice the economy. Never mind that the $830 billion Obama
economic stimulus didn't work to create jobs (see Figure 5.2) The
more government spent, the more the unemployment rate remained
stubbornly stuck at above 8 percent.

But the real lesson of the failed Keynesian spending model
comes from the other side of the pond—in Europe, which at the time
of this writing is still in financial turmoil. Greece, Portugal, Spain,
and other big-spending European nations are imploding with
unemployment rates soaring. The EU has had to intervene with a $1
trillion bailout that keeps getting bigger each month. If there is any
good that can come from the Greek calamity—that could spread to
other nations in Europe—it is that we are witnessing firsthand the
corrosive consequences of the economic theories of Mr. Keynes.

Princeton economist Alan Blinder once described the theory
behind this policy prescription by writing that public sector
spending causes a "multiplier effect; that is, output increases by

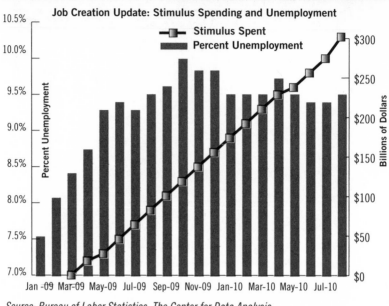

Figure 5.3: The Stimulus and Jobs

Job Creation Update: Stimulus Spending and Unemployment

Source: Bureau of Labor Statistics, The Center for Data Analysis.

a multiple of the original change in spending that caused it." Last year, some economists predicted that every dollar of debt-funded government spending could magically lead to $2 or $3 of new private activity. Remember, the Obama administration said this when it promised three million jobs "saved or created" from its failed $830 billion stimulus package.

Countries were urged to throw fiscal caution to the wind. In its *Economic Outlook* published in November 2008, the International Monetary Fund, which is the international agency whose mission is to prevent economic panics, advised member nations like Greece: "There is a clear need for additional macroeconomic policy stimulus relative to what has been announced thus far, to support growth and provide a context to restore health to financial sectors." At its February 2009 emergency "Group of 20" meetings, the IMF economists advised "aggressive" pedal-to-the-metal government spending "to resolve the crisis." The IMF continued that "a key feature of a fiscal stimulus program is that it should support demand for *a prolonged period of time* and be applied broadly across countries," (emphasis ours). IMF officials also lectured that the global risk was that government borrowing would be too small, not too large. In other words, give the alcoholic another drink.

The United States, Germany, France, Ireland, Spain, and almost all OECD nations took that advice to heart, but perhaps no nation more so than Greece, which employed Keynesianism on steroids. Greek debt as a share of GDP skyrocketed to 116 percent from an already high 85 percent of GDP in 2007, as the socialist government promised voters more public sector hiring, more generous benefits (such as fourteen months of pay for twelve months of work), and more subsidies to ailing industries.

We hasten to mention that most of the other nations in Europe that are on the potential contamination list—Ireland, Italy, Portugal, and Spain—also dutifully passed textbook Keynesian spending stimulus plans and their debt to GDP levels also soared. In 2010 the Italian debt hit 118 percent and the Portuguese debt was nearly 90 percent and climbing. Spain's 2009 deficit soared to 11 percent of GDP and Ireland's to 14 percent. Just what the Keynesian witch doctors ordered.

Now in Greece unemployment is rising rapidly, output has crashed, and interest rates have more than quadrupled on its sovereign debt that is now considered toxic. Keynesian economics has gone haywire. The rapid deterioration of Greek debt is a painful but useful lesson that debt financing of runaway government spending is anything but free, and it's hardly something to only worry about, as Lord Keynes himself famously put it, "in the long run" when "we are all dead." Instead, we're witnessing in Greece that runaway government spending can derail a national economy with the suddenness and ferocity of a thunderbolt. Mr. Keynes and his disciples never counted on the punishing force of modern day bond vigilantes.

Now we have an astonishing twist in the story. The "emergency" rescue plan imposed on Greece and concocted by many of the same economists who advised that nation to spend, spend, spend just eighteen months ago, is for "austerity." The IMF/European Union has commanded Greece to cut government budgets, slash pensions and payrolls, raise the VAT tax to 21 or even 23 percent (from 19 percent at the start of the year), to forestall a financial meltdown. In other words, never mind our earlier counsel to run up the credit card; what is needed now is less debt and less consumption/demand. Huh? The politicians in Greece, all of Europe, and here, can be excused if they're complaining of policy whiplash from the contradictory advice they are getting from Keyensian scholars.

Some of the Keynesians are seeking—as they watch the destructive consequences brought on by their own dismal advice of 2008 and 2009—an abandonment or devaluation of the Euro currency, so that debt-deluged nations like Greece can repay or repudiate their sovereign debt. Of course, a currency revaluation will only incite inflation, which, we should have learned in the 1970s, causes rapid acceleration in interest rates on government bonds—so this solution is at best self-defeating. The experiences of nations like Argentina, Bolivia, and Mexico should have taught that lesson.

Keynesians defend their contradictory advice by explaining that what they meant for countries like Greece, Ireland, Portugal, and the United States was temporary debt-fueled government stimulus followed by medium term progress to restore balanced budgets. But even if plausible in theory, this has always been a fantasy in the real world. Giving politicians like Nancy Pelosi and Gordon Brown the green light to spend money irresponsibly is like giving a pyromaniac a blowtorch. In Washington, DC, European capitals' government spending programs are never temporary.

The U.S. Congress still hasn't ended stimulus programs that date back to the New Deal era of the 1930s and already stimulus plans from 2009 are being extended. Keynesianism has always been an intellectual hoax, an excuse to ratchet up government power and reach, and to redistribute income in the here and now, and pay the bills later by raising taxes. Exhibit A is the Obama administration's plan to raise tax rates on investment across the board in 2013 in part to pay for the $830 billion spending stimulus passed in 2009. Apparently, there are no negative multiplier effects to tax increases.

Keynesianism is also crumbling before our very eyes because the promised recovery in jobs in the United States and Europe has simply not materialized. The economic rebound in Europe from colossal government borrowing has only brought on a new round of financial turmoil. The nations with the most debt are getting clobbered in global markets, as capital flees these nations. Japan since 1991 should have been the showcase for the Keynesian canard, as the Japanese governments have unsuccessfully launched at least five "stimulus" plans over the past twenty years, even as Japan's stock market has lost two-thirds of its value. Even the Obama administration was forced to concede that its stimulus was a failure when it agreed to extend supply side tax rate cuts at the end of 2010. It was an admission that spending stimulus had failed.

The Keynesian response to the observable failures of its policies is to call for even more stimulus, except, of course, when the stimulus is too much—as in Greece.

John Maynard Keynes once said that politicians who pursue wrong-headed policy prescriptions "are usually the slave of some defunct economist." The defunct and derailed idea of Keynesianism is at the center of the panic in Europe. It threatens to shift the U.S. economy into a lower gear for many years to come. Its application has placed governments across the globe in deeper levels of debt than at any time since the end of World War II. The global capital markets won't tolerate that much longer, and even the Keynesians of Europe are recognizing that reality—when will U.S. politicians in the states, cities, and Washington?

CHAPTER 6

SOAK THE RICH WITH LOWER TAX RATES

When men get in the habit of helping themselves to
the property of others, they cannot easily be cured of it.
—New York Times, 1909

O ne of the most amazing political transformations in modern
times is how the two political parties, Republicans and
Democrats, have switched positions on tax policy.
Back in the 1960s it was Republicans who complained
that President Kennedy's tax cuts were "fiscally irresponsible"
and would increase the budget deficit to intolerable levels, and
Democrats who argued for the sanity of lower tax rates to grow the
economy. Amazingly, it was Republican icons and future presidential
candidates Barry Goldwater and Bob Dole who in 1964 voted *against*
reducing the tax rate from 91 to 70 percent. Of course, it was President
Kennedy himself who was the most eloquent in dismissing the tax-cut
naysayers when he pronounced: "Our true choice is not between tax
reduction, on the one hand, and the avoidance of large federal deficits
on the other...It is between two kinds of deficits—a chronic deficit
of inertia, as the unwanted result of inadequate revenues and a
restricted economy—or a temporary deficit of transition, resulting
from a tax cut designed to boost the economy, produce revenues, and
achieve a future budget surplus. The first type of deficit is a sign of
waste and weakness—the second reflects an investment in the future."
Well said and still quite true today.

It's striking that the Kennedy tax cutting legacy has become an
embarrassment to 21st century liberals, even those who trumpet
the Camelot years, the success of the Kennedy presidency, and the
resiliency of his ideas. John F. Kennedy was a pro-growth tax cutter.

Figure 6.1: Lower Tax Rates in the 1920s Meant More Tax Revenue

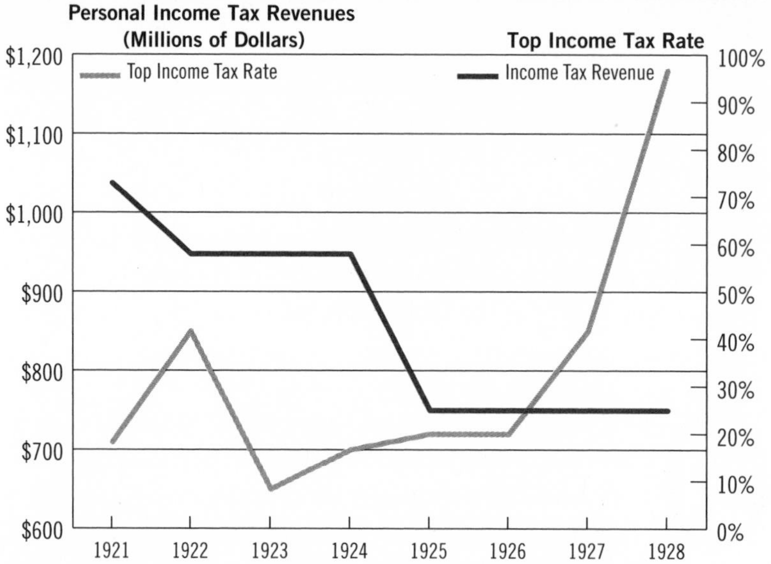

Personal Income Tax Revenues
(Millions of Dollars)   Top Income Tax Rate

Legend: Top Income Tax Rate; Income Tax Revenue

Source: Tax Foundation; Joint Economic Committee, "The Mellon and Kennedy Tax Cuts: A Review and Analysis," Staff Study, June 18, 1982

The best way to grow the economy, he argued, as Ronald Reagan did later, "is to reduce the burden on private income and the deterrents to private initiative which are imposed by our present tax system— and this administration is pledged to an across-the-board reduction in personal and corporate income tax cuts." Republicans starting with Reagan stole that line in 1980.

WHAT HISTORY TEACHES US ABOUT THE LAFFER CURVE
In the last hundred years there have been four episodes of significant tax rate reductions. These reductions occurred in the 1920s under Presidents Warren Harding and Calvin Coolidge; in the 1960s under President John F. Kennedy; in the 1980s under President Reagan; and in the early 2000s under George W. Bush. In each case the tax cuts were predicted to lose revenues, but instead federal revenues increased after the tax rates were cut because the economy responded positively to the lower tax rate regime.

HARDING-COOLIDGE TAX CUTS

Although the United States briefly instituted an income tax during the Civil War, the Supreme Court struck this act and other income taxes down throughout the 19th century. It was not until 1913 with the passage of the 16th Amendment to the Constitution that the income tax became a permanent fixture of government in America. This was a black chapter in American history. The *New York Times*, yes, the *New York Times*, long opposed an income tax, even writing in 1894 (when Congress tried to enact one) that that this would be a "vicious, inequitable, unpopular, impolitic, and socialist act." The tax, argued the *New York Times*, was "the most unreasoning and un-American movement in the politics of the last quarter century."

And even the *Washington Post* saw the negative effects on work and effort from a graduated income tax. "It is an abhorrent and calamitous monstrosity," the *Post* editorial board seethed. "It punishes everyone who rises above the rank of mediocrity. The fewer additional yokes put around the neck of labor the better." If only the Congress believed that today.

The tax was supposed to be capped at no higher than 7 percent and it was only supposed to apply to the very richest Americans: the Rockefellers and the Vanderbilts. When the income tax amendment was debated some of the opponents in Congress argued that there should be a constitutional cap on income tax at 10 percent. But the income tax supporters assured voters that there would never been an income tax rate that high, so this protection was not necessary. Whether they knew it or not, they couldn't have been more wrong about the future of the income tax.

Within just eight years of the first income tax over the course Woodrow Wilson's presidency, the top tax rate stood at not 7 percent, but 73 percent by 1921. The tax rate increases were said to be justified to raise the revenue needed to fight the Germans in World War I. In the 1920 presidential election the Republicans promised a "return to normalcy" and Warren Harding was elected in a landslide. The country was suffering a post-war recession, and unemployment soared. Harding, and then after he died in office, his successor Calvin Coolidge, promoted a steep reduction in tax rates to get the U.S. economy moving again.

The Harding-Coolidge tax rate reductions brought the top income tax rate down in stages from the wartime high of 73 percent in 1921 to 25 percent in 1925. This was the largest reduction in tax rates on the wealthy in American history. Coolidge argued for the reductions in his 1924 State of the Union address by reminding the public that "when the taxation of large incomes is excessive they tend to disappear." He confidently predicted that his plan "would actually yield more revenues to the government if the basis of taxation were scientifically revised downward."

He was proven remarkably correct. The economy roared back to life in the mid-1920s and the nation's greatest period of prosperity up until that time replaced recession. Happy days were here again and America's industrial production surged back to full throttle. These were the Roaring '20s, when America reached new levels of affluence never seen before. Babe Ruth made a salary of $100,000 a year—for playing baseball and for achieving the unthinkable: swatting sixty home runs in a single season. It was indeed a gilded age, the era of *The Great Gatsby.* The rich got unbelievably rich, but as per capita income soared, a joyful prosperity spread like a gale force wind across the nation. More and more middle class Americans gained a level of affluence that was unthinkable in earlier times. The middle class and even many of the poor could afford radios and plumbing and hot water and trips to the movies.

How much of this prosperity was a direct result of tax cuts is not exactly clear and still to this day a subject of debate. But what is undeniably true is that tax revenues increased even as tax rates fell. Between 1923 and 1928 real tax collections nearly doubled as the economy surged. Figure 6.1 shows that as the tax rates were chopped by almost two-thirds, the share of taxes paid by those earning over $50,000 (the rich back then), rose from 45 percent in 1921 when the rate was 73 percent to 62 percent in 1925 when their rate was 25 percent. Those who made more than $100,000 a year saw their tax share rise from 28 percent to 51 percent. Total tax revenues rose from $720 million in 1921 to $1.15 billion by 1928. There was no long term loss of revenue from the tax rate cut.

President Calvin Coolidge—"keep cool with Cal"—pushed hard for the tax cuts, and made eloquent speeches on how tax rate cuts would spur greater output and employment. Sounding much like Reagan and Kennedy to come, he said in 1924: "Experience does not show that the higher rate produces the larger revenue. Experience is all the other way."

There is no escaping that when the taxation of large incomes is excessive, they tend to disappear.

I agree perfectly with those who wish to relieve the small taxpayer by getting the largest possible contribution from the people with large incomes. But if the rates on large incomes are so high that they disappear, the small taxpayer will be left with the entire burden. If, on the other hand, the rates are placed where they will produce the most revenue from large incomes, then the small taxpayer will be relieved.

One of the main architects behind this first American supply side tax cut was Secretary of the Treasury Andrew Mellon. (Sometimes the '20s tax plan is called the "Mellon tax cuts.") Mellon, arguably the greatest treasury secretary of the 20th century, was one of the few people in Washington or on Wall Street who predicted that lowering the tax rates would produce more growth and even more revenue. "It seems difficult for people to understand," he said of the tax cuts, "that high rates of taxation do not necessarily mean large revenues to the government and that more revenue may often be obtained by lower tax rates." He continued by educating that when tax rates were as high as they were in the early 1920s, "a decrease in taxes causes an inspiration to trade and commerce, which increases the prosperity of the country so that revenues of the government, even on a lower basis of tax, are increased."

In the fall of 1929, the stock market crashed and the economy toppled down as wealth evaporated.

One contributor to the crash was the reversal of the Coolidge tax rate cuts. In Herbert Hoover's last year in office, as the economy continued to sag, the federal government faced a $2 billion budget deficit. Hoover and Republicans in Congress called for a tax increase enacting the Revenue Act of 1932. Tax rates more than doubled. The economy sunk. Franklin Delano Roosevelt entered office and raised tax rates up to 63 percent from 25 percent. All the rates were raised. FDR and the Democrats increased the gift and estate taxes to stick it to the rich. Then in 1935, FDR increased the top tax rate to more than 79 percent, then 83 percent, and then during the war, to an astounding 92 percent. Workers and investors kept eight cents on the dollar.

THE KENNEDY TAX CUTS

America's high tax rates took a toll. The economy grew in the 1950s, but in fits and starts, and by the end of the Eisenhower presidency, the economy was stalled again. A young, successful actor of that era, Ronald Reagan, would later recall while campaigning for president that with tax rates of 90 percent, once you were in that highest tax bracket you stopped working; stopped making movies; stopped activity that would give ninety cents of every dollar earned to the government.

John F. Kennedy ran for president promising to spend more money on defense to close "the missile gap," and to get the economy growing faster. "We can do bettah," was the famous catch phrase from the young and charismatic Massachusetts Senator. In 1960 the Democratic Party's theme was growth and more growth. The 1960 Democratic national platform called for the achievement of 5 percent real economic growth rates—something we wish either party today would strive for.

When Kennedy took office in 1961, the highest federal tax rate at the margin was 91 percent. The lowest was 20 percent. Many of Kennedy's advisers, including John Kenneth Galbraith, argued for a massive government spending program to induce more demand and create more jobs. But Kennedy was ultimately his own counselor on economics and he understood human nature and the lessons of history. He decided that the way to get the American economy shifting into a higher gear was through across the board reductions in taxation.

Kennedy made it very clear early on that he had an innate understanding of the policies that nurture and reward growth. He was the first modern-day supply side president. Here's what he said in the 1963 *Economic Report of the President:*

Yet many taxpayers seemed prepared to deny the nation the fruits of tax reduction because they question the financial soundness of reducing taxes when the federal budget is already in deficit. Let me make clear why, in today's economy, fiscal prudence and responsibility call for tax reduction even if it temporarily enlarged the federal deficit—why reducing taxes is the best way open to us to increase revenues.

Tragically, President Kennedy was assassinated a few months before his tax cut package was enacted into law in early 1964. The tax cuts reduced the maximum marginal personal income tax rate from 91 percent to 70 percent by 1965 and the lower rates were chopped as well.

By the way, when an economist refers to the "tax rate at the margin," or "marginal tax rate," he (or she) means the amount of tax you pay on the *last* dollar you earn. Our income tax is progressive, which means that it starts low and gets higher as your income goes up. A worker earning $25,000 a year pays a lower tax rate than an executive who makes $100,000 a year. The lower rate may start at, say, 20 percent on the first $50,000, then rises to 35 percent on the next $50,000, and so on. So if you make over $100,000, any money you earn above that amount will be taxed at the marginal, or highest, rate you have achieved.

When some of his opponents suggested that this tax cut would benefit the rich, Kennedy dismissed this claim, arguing that economic growth would benefit people of all incomes. As President Kennedy put it: "A rising tide lifts all boats."

The tax cut was debated for months in the halls of Congress—and ironically this was a tax cut agenda that Republicans almost universally opposed and Democrats almost universally favored (as we've seen, politics has since flipped itself on its head). One of the most vocal supporters of the policy was House Ways and Means Committee chairman Wilbur Mills. His speech on the floor of the House is worth repeating, because here was one of the most prominent and economically respected Democrats arguing that this tax cut would *raise revenue:*

> *Mr. Chairman, there is no doubt in my mind that this tax*
> *reduction bill, in and of itself, can bring about an increase in the gross*
> *national product of approximately $50 billion in the next few years. If*
> *it does, these lower rates of taxation will bring in at least 12 billion in*
> *additional revenue.*

Then Mr. Mills prophesied that because of additional economic growth from the tax cut, "the larger revenues derived from this additional income will result in the federal budget being balanced sooner than would be the case in the absence of the tax cut." There is almost no Democrat who believes that to be true today.

The Kennedy tax cut was enacted in 1964. Although Kennedy did not live to see it, he was (as Mills was) proven right in his prediction that the American economic engines would roar to life if taxes were less oppressive. The economy grew rapidly in 1964, '65, and '66. The unemployment rate fell to its lowest peacetime level in more than thirty years. "The unusual budget spectacle of sharply rising revenues following the biggest tax cut in history," announced a 1966 *U.S. News and World Report* article, "is beginning to astonish even those who pushed hardest for tax cuts in the first place." No kidding. Arthur Okun, who was President Lyndon Johnson's chief economic adviser, calculated a massive stimulus from the plan: "The tax cuts of 1964 are credited with a $25 billion contribution to our GNP by mid-1965, a $30 billion effect by the end of 1965, and an ultimate $36 billion increment." Remember: This was 1966 when the U.S. economy was about one-fifth as large as today, so $36 billion was a more than a 10 percent addition to national output.

Even more shocking was the impact on the distribution of taxes paid. Lower tax rates on the rich led to these income classes paying a much larger share of the tax burden. Americans earning over $50,000 per year (the equivalent of about $200,000 today) increased their taxes by nearly 40 percent after the rate cut. Their tax share rose from 12 percent of the total in 1963 to almost 15 percent in 1966. See Figure 6.2. Americans with an income of more than $1 million nearly doubled their tax payments from $311 million in 1962 when the tax rate was 91 percent to $603 million in 1965 when the tax rate was 70 percent.

Figure 6.2: The Rich Paid More Under Kennedy Tax Cuts

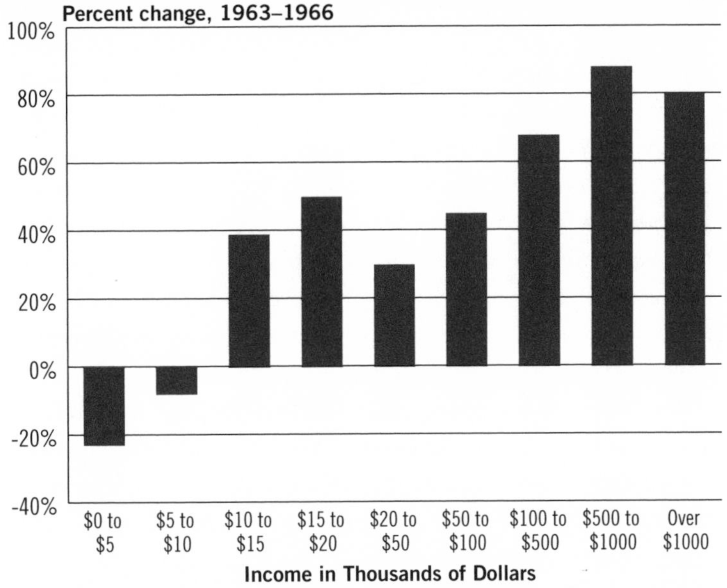

Percent change, 1963–1966

Income in Thousands of Dollars

Source: Tax Foundation; Joint Economic Committee, "The Mellon and Kennedy Tax Cuts: A Review and Analysis," Staff Study, June 18, 1982

There are other sets of statistics that support the effect of the tax cut on subsequent revenues but this isn't an economic text so we won't include them here. Walter Heller, who had served as President Kennedy's Chairman of the Council of Economic Advisers, summed it all up neatly in his testimony before Congress in 1977:

> *What happened to the tax cut in 1965 is difficult to pin down, but insofar as we are able to isolate it, it did seem to have a tremendously stimulative effect, a multiplied effect on the economy. It was the major factor that led to our running a $3 billion surplus by the middle of 1965 before escalation in Vietnam struck us. It was a $12 billion tax cut, which would be about $33 or $34 billion in today's terms, and within one year the revenues into the Federal Treasury were already above what they had been before the tax cut.*

Did the tax cut pay for itself in increased revenues? I think the evidence is very strong that it did.

THE REAGAN-KEMP TAX CUTS

Ronald Reagan and Congressman Jack Kemp from Buffalo were about the only two politicians who were paying attention. Reagan's tax cuts were modeled after the Kennedy plan. Tax rates were cut across the board (the original Reagan idea was for a 30 percent tax rate cut, which was scaled back to 25 percent). The highest tax rate was slashed from 70 percent to 50 percent and then later to 28 percent. Now it was Republicans arguing for lower tax rates and Democrats arguing this could not be afforded.

The economy soared in the 1980s and the unemployment rate plunged after the mini-depression of 1978–1982. Tax revenues also surged after the tax rate cuts. From 1980 to 1990 total federal revenues doubled in nominal terms from $517 billion to $1,032 billion, a 30 percent increase after inflation.

Whether or not the income tax cuts paid for themselves is an open question and almost beside the point. But what is beyond debate is that taxes paid by the wealthiest Americans facing the highest marginal tax rates increased every year during the '80s expansion. The increase in tax payments at the high end of the income scale were an astonishing instant replay of the effects of the Kennedy tax cuts. The rich paid more after the income tax rate cuts in 1981.

In constant dollars, the richest 10 percent of Americans paid $177 billion in federal income taxes in 1980 but paid $237 billion in 1988. The remaining 90 percent of households paid $5 billion less in income taxes over this period. [1] The wealthy earned more and they paid more. In fact, Federal Reserve Board member Lawrence Lindsey has shown in the peer-reviewed *Journal of Public Economics* that taxes paid by the wealthy were substantially higher than they

---

1 William A. Niskansen and Stephen Moore, "Supply-Side Tax Cuts and the Truth about the Reagan Economic Record," *Policy Analysis*, October 22, 1996. http://www.cato.org/publications/policy-analysis/supplyside-tax-cuts-truth-about-reagan-economic-record

would have been if the top tax rate had remained at 70 percent. [2] Lindsey painstakingly compared how much revenues were generated by the tax cuts with what revenues were expected to be without them. He finds that for *all* of Reagan's income tax cuts, between one-sixth and one-quarter of the expected revenue loss was "recouped by changes in taxpayer behavior." He estimated that federal revenues would be maximized by an income tax rate of between 35 and 40 percent. But what was most remarkable about Lindsey's findings was that the tax cuts for the richest Americans *raised* revenues:

> *A comparison of the predicted level of revenues with the actual taxes paid shows that about $17.8 billion more was collected than predicted. Nearly all this revenue response could be found in the top taxpayer group. These taxpayers actually paid $42.1 billion in taxes compared with the $27 billion predicted. As in 1982 and 1983, the actual taxes paid by these taxpayers was more than predicted would have been paid under the old tax law.*

Lindsey concluded his analysis on the Reagan tax cuts by stating:

> *Some of the more extreme supply-side hypotheses were proven false. But the core supply side tenet — that tax rates powerfully affect the willingness of taxpayers to work, save and invest, and thereby also affect the health of the economy — won as stunning a vindication as have been seen in at least a half-century of economics.*

Figure 6.3 shows that the share of total income taxes paid by the wealthiest 1 percent of all Americans actually rose from 18 percent in 1981 to 25 percent in 1990. The wealthiest 5 percent of Americans saw their tax share rise from 35 to 44 percent. So the rise in the deficit was clearly not a result of "tax cuts for the rich" but a rise in federal expenditures.

---

2 Ibid.

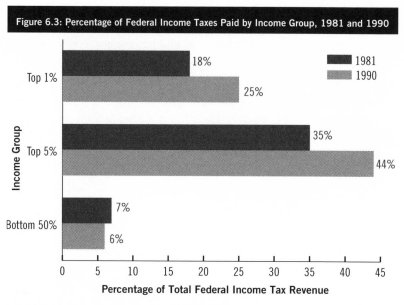

Figure 6.3: Percentage of Federal Income Taxes Paid by Income Group, 1981 and 1990

Source: Tax Foundation, "Tax Features," August 1992.

George W. Bush Tax Cuts

This tax rate cutting history would not be complete without a quick summary of the last part of the story: the Bush investment tax cuts of 2003. That plan reduced the income, capital gains, and dividend tax rates to spur a stock market recovery and a growth in jobs. Mr. Bush was accused of employing trickle-down economics and of installing a tax cut philosophy that would not work to revive the economy. The lion's share of the tax cuts were to be directed to the rich, and the poor and middle class would get a penny in relief for every dollar the super rich received. Here in a nutshell were the results:

· Tax receipts exploded by a record $700 billion from 2003-2007.
· The economy produced eight million new jobs.
· Most impressive, and once again, the rich paid more tax, not less. The latest Treasury Department data examines the distribution of federal taxes by income group and is shown in Table 6.1. It shows the highest proportion of the income tax shouldered by the very

richest Americans ever in 2005 *after the Bush tax cuts*. The top 1 percent earn 21 percent of the income but pay 39 percent of the income tax and the top 10 percent pay 67 percent of the tab. The bottom 50 percent, those below the median income in America now earn 13.5 percent of the income and pay just 3 percent of the taxes.

Table 6.1: Who Paid How Much in Taxes in 2005		
	Share of Income	Share of Federal Income Taxes
Top 1%	21	39
Top 5%	33	57
Top 10%	44	66
Top 25%	66	85
Bottom 50%	13	3

THE DEBATE RAGES ON

But the debate never ends. Now the entire discussion is on the alleged benefits of raising tax rates again and repealing the lower rates enacted under Mr. Bush. Is Barack Obama the Democrats' Herbert Hoover? He sounds like him and has the same prescriptions: Soak the rich and our problems will go away. We've lived through that already and the results were catastrophic.

The normal response to this history is that Bill Clinton raised tax rates and the economy boomed. It is true that the last six Clinton years were very prosperous, even after the top tax rate rose to 36.9 percent from 31 percent. But my view is, other Clinton policies that were pro-growth counteracted the rise in tax rates. Mr. Clinton cut government spending from 22 percent to 18 percent of GDP, enacted welfare reform, and cut the capital gains tax rate to 15 percent from 20 percent. It was Bill Clinton who declared in 1996 that, "The era of big government is over." And for too short a while, it was.

CHAPTER 7

WHY FLAT IS FAIR

Rather than raising tax rates in 2013, maybe, just maybe, there is a different consensus brewing on tax policy. Senate Democrat Max Baucus, the Senate Finance Committee Chairman, recently declared that we need to fix and reform the current tax code with lower rates and more deductions. Hooray.

And even class warrior Barack Obama acknowledged in early 2012 that the problems with the current tax code are manifold. The U.S. "statutory tax rate will soon be the highest among advanced countries" he says. And that the "relatively narrow tax base and a high statutory tax rate [means that] the U.S. tax system is uncompetitive and inefficient." (Maybe he's been reading the *Wall Street Journal* editorial pages after all.) The White House corporate tax reform proposal is also right that the tax code is too dependent on debt financing, rather than equity financing (a bias the president will make *worse* by raising capital gains and dividend taxes). But let's focus on the positive and the point of near universal agreement on the left and right: This tax code is an abomination that is not fair or pro-growth. How do we fix it? The answer is the flat tax.

THE HONG KONG TAX MIRACLE

My favorite example of a flat rate tax system is that of Hong Kong. Hong Kong adopted a 15 percent flat tax fifty years ago and has been a glittering model of tax efficiency and sanity ever since. This island is now one of the wealthiest places on the globe thanks in part to low tax rates and tax simplicity. There was worry when Hong Kong was given back to China that the flat tax would be swallowed up by the Chinese tax system. Just the opposite has occurred. The genetic capitalistic impulse of the Chinese has led the mainland to move toward the Hong Kong system through tax rate reductions and saving and investment incentives. Even Russia—the home of communism—now has converted to a 13 percent flat tax and it gets more revenue than it did when rates were above 50 percent.

What Should a Fair Tax Code Do?

First, we have taxes to raise revenues to pay for government services. That means, most vitally, paying for our national defense, but also for police and fire workers, building roads, parks, and other public facilities, funding services like the FBI and the CIA, and paying the millions of people who work for the government, from the diplomats who serve as ambassadors abroad, to the social workers who help the poor and needy. The government also spends enormous amounts of money to provide services to the elderly, the retired, the poor, our veterans, and others. Few would argue with the need to pay taxes to fund activities that are for the collective good. Here is where we encounter some major differences of opinion about how much the government should do.

A tax system at least should raise money efficiently. Ours doesn't. In 2008 and 2009 federal tax receipts averaged barely 15 percent of GDP. With spending closer to 25 percent of GDP, that doesn't work. With a pro-growth tax code, we could have a tax system that raised between 18 and 20 percent of GDP—that is far more than today, and with *lower* tax rates.

Second, taxes are increasingly used to redistribute income from rich to poor. We've swung way too far in the direction of using the tax code for redistribution purposes, but a flat tax can be devised in a way to protect the poor from high taxes. And if we want to help the poor, the best way to do that is not through the tax code.

Third, the tax code is used to regulate behavior, to reward certain activities and to punish others. This is social engineering via the tax system. It is what we need to stop doing. We cattle-prod people with tax breaks for everything from giving money to the Girl Scouts, to buying a home, to paying for college tuition, to buying energy efficient refrigerators and washers and dryers. And then we punish them for activities we don't approve of. Even if you don't smoke, you are likely aware that taxes on cigarettes are very high. Likewise alcohol. Sometimes we perversely penalize activities that we view as virtuous. Through dividend taxes, estate taxes, capital gains taxes, and the like, we double- and triple-tax people on savings—then Congress complains Americans aren't saving enough.

We would want a tax system to be simple and efficient, but clearly ours isn't. It was Albert Einstein who said the most complicated thing in the universe is the U.S. federal income tax code. Things are getting worse. We have added five thousand changes to the tax code in just the last ten years.

Today we have undoubtedly the most complex and incomprehensible tax code in the world. The Internal Revenue Service employs 115,000 people, has an annual budget of $11 billion, and is the largest federal bureaucracy. The IRS sends out eight billion pages of forms and instructions each year. Laid end to end, they would stretch around the earth twenty-eight times. This can't be good for the economy or the environment. (Think of all the trees we need to cut down to produce all that paper.) Figure 7.1 shows the growth in the number of words in the internal revenue code.

All of this complexity means lots of work for tax lobbyists and accountants who make big dollars to puncture holes in the tax code and to help their clients find clever and (mostly) legal ways to minimize their tax payments. Firms like H & R Block and the other big accounting firms do billions of dollars of business a year—and, by the way, these companies are some of the biggest opponents of the flat tax.

The higher the tax rate, the greater the value of special interest loopholes and carve-outs and the more coveted lobbyists become. Think about it: At a 40 percent tax rate a tax deduction is worth twice what a tax deduction is at a 20 percent tax rate. This is something that Barack Obama does not seem to understand. He says he wants to get rid of the special interest influences and the corporate lobbyists who get Hershey's Kisses from Congress for their clients, but by raising tax rates to 50 percent or more, he makes lobbyists a prized commodity. Why not put these parasites out of business?

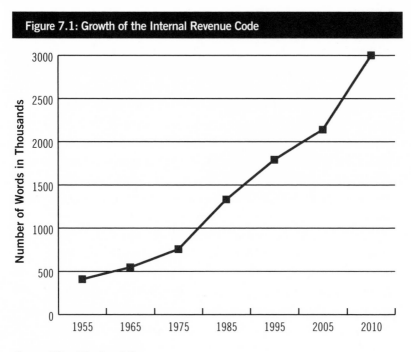

Figure 7.1: Growth of the Internal Revenue Code

Source: IRS and Tax Foundation

WHAT'S FAIR AND WHAT ISN'T

What isn't fair is the current code. It is patently unfair is that two people can live right across the street from each other, have the same income, the same four-bedroom home, the same number of children, and the same lifestyle, but one pays three or four times more tax than the other. The one takes clever advantage of every deduction and loophole he and his accountant can find; the other doesn't do any tax planning or sheltering of income. The point is our tax code violates the principle of treating all people equally under the law. The tax code creates inequality. Warren Buffett claims his taxes are too low, but he takes advantage of tax loopholes.

Now assume we have a flat tax of, say, 19 percent. That would be a tax on all of your income regardless of source. There will be no deductions except for family size. In this scenario, the fellow who makes $100,000 a year pays $19,000 in taxes, and the other gal who makes $100,000 a year pays $19,000 in taxes. Each pays the same tax.

The guy in the mansion who makes $1 million a year pays $190,000 in taxes. (For simplicity, this ignores that the flat tax would probably include a deduction for oneself and children)

But there are plenty of politicians who believe that the earner who makes $1 million a year should pay *more* than ten times what the fellow who makes ten times less pays. These folks think that the richer fellow should be taxed at a higher rate. Why? Because we are told that they can afford to pay more. But the point of this book is demonstrate time and again that the impact of these higher tax rates is merely to discourage these rich people from working, investing, saving, and taking risks to start businesses. And we have tried to show that these ever higher tax rates wind up hurting everyone by damaging the productive capacity of the U.S. economy.

Flatten It

There have been many attempts to institute a flat tax over the years. None has succeeded, although in 1986 Congress eliminated some loopholes and lowered rates to 28 percent. One reason for the lack of success is that many of the earlier attempts at a flat tax were piecemeal approaches which tended to address a specific tax and leave others in place. This approach will never succeed. To succeed, true tax reform works best if it takes into account the entire tax code, not bits and pieces of it.

What Is the Flat Tax Rate?

Changes to marginal tax rates are critical for growth because they change incentives to demand, and to supply, work effort, and capital. Firms base their decisions to employ workers, in part, on the workers' total cost to the firm. Holding all else equal, the greater the cost to the firm of employing each additional worker, the fewer workers the firm will employ. Conversely, the lower the marginal cost per worker, the more workers the firm will hire. For the firm, the decision to employ is based upon gross wages paid, a concept which encompasses all costs borne by the firm.

So we want a rate that is below 20 percent, that is applicable to everyone, and that does not double and triple tax savings and investment. (No death tax.) The plan could exempt the first $20,000 of income for a family of four so as to add some progressivity and spare poor people from getting hit with a tax bill. If we had such a system, the United States would go overnight from being one of the highest tax rate nations to one of the lowest. This means more jobs, more capital, and more tax revenues for the government. The simplicity of a postcard return will mean billions of hours not wasted on tax returns at the corporate and individual tax level.

To create a fairer society, there is no alternative to economic growth. And a tax system that destroys jobs and wealth is the most regressive tax of all. That is why flat is fair.

Abolish the Corporate Tax

What about the corporate income tax? I have a radical idea. Abolish it. This would eliminate the facade that corporations pay taxes (they merely collect them), and would let the taxes be paid by the owners— rich, middle class, and poor—when they receive the income. This would be a blow for real tax fairness because it would help establish the equity principle that all income should be taxed at the federal level one time and only one time.

Abolishing the federal corporate tax would solve myriad other problems that arise from this tax. Economists at the OECD reported in 2008 that high corporate taxes have the most negative impact on incomes and growth of all taxes. "Corporate income taxes appear to have a particularly negative impact on GDP per capita," the study concluded. The Tax Foundation recently reported that because of reductions in corporate tax rates around the globe over these same twenty-five years, the U.S. rate (federal plus state) of 39 percent is about half again as high as the international average. This operates like a self-defeating tariff on our own goods.

Mr. Obama's own tax reform panel, chaired by Paul Volcker, found that the "growing gap between the U.S. corporate tax rate and the corporate tax rates of most other countries generates incentives for U.S. corporations to shift their income and operations to foreign locations to lower corporate tax rates to avoid U.S. rates." As nations around the world have cut their rates, the report warns, "these incentives have become stronger." The Bowles-Simpson bipartisan commission largely agreed, arguing that the current corporate tax "puts U.S. corporations at a competitive disadvantage against their foreign competitors." That's a near unanimous conclusion these days, and you'd be hard pressed to find any reputable economists who disagree with that premise.

Eliminating the corporate tax doesn't just benefit the 100 million or so American shareholders. It will also benefit middle class workers. A study by Kevin Hassett and Aparna Mathur of the American Enterprise Institute reviewed manufacturing wages in seventy-two nations from 1981 to 2003 and found that because the corporate tax reduces capital investment in the United States, and thus lowers worker productivity, a 1 percent increase in the corporate tax causes wages to fall by between 0.8 percent and 1 percent. AFL-CIO president Richard Trumka should be paying attention.

The corporate tax is also among the least cost-efficient taxes levied by the federal government. In 2011 the corporate income tax raised $192 billion. But companies paid an estimated $40 billion— or more than twenty cents on the dollar—in legal, accounting, and bookkeeping costs to figure out how much they owe. Many companies incur compliance costs in the millions of dollars but pay no tax at all. What's the point?

There's a strong case for eliminating this burdensome tax entirely, but we'll admit it isn't very realistic given the current political alignment in Washington. That said, this may be a moment when both parties can prove the cynics wrong, crack through the political gridlock, and agree on significant rate reduction for the good of the country. "How low you can go" in cutting rates, says Treasury Secretary Tim Geithner, "depends on how much of the reform you can achieve." That means closing corporate loopholes, which makes sense and is a lobbyist's nightmare.

FLAT, FAIR, AND SIMPLE

The ideas presented here—the flat tax and the abolition of the corporate tax—are admittedly bold and daring. But times of economic and fiscal crisis are the right moments for big and seismic changes in the way our government operates. We need a redesigned tax code engineered for growth, competitiveness, and prosperity. The rest of the world is moving that way; if we don't change, they may catch up to us. We can't stand still—and we can't stand pat. Raising tax rates on production and work and effort and entrepreneurship will only shift the U.S. economy in reverse. By contrast, the tax reforms outlined here would create that "rising tide" that JFK spoke of that "lifts all boats." And that is why the flat tax is the fairest of them all.

Acknowledgments

I wish to thank my friend, mentor, and often co-author Arthur Laffer for his kind comments and suggestions on an early draft. Thanks also to Tyler Grimm for all his expert research assistance and Frances McCloskey for her editorial help. I would also like to thank James Piereson and Thomas W. Smith for their help. Katherine Wong at Encounter was a terrific editor and Roger Kimball helped launch the project and bring it to Encounter. My friends Peter Morse, Dick and Mary Beth Weiss, Jerry Milbank, Carl Helstrom, Peter Ferrara, James Piereson, Thomas W. Smith, Richard and Sherry Sharp, Ford Scudder and Ken Cribb were invaluable advisors.